Soul Care

70 Inspirational Notes to Connect with God and Self

Tony L. Warrick

Soul Care
Copyright © 2021 by Tony L. Warrick

All rights reserved. This book or parts thereof may not be reproduced in any form, stored in any retrieval system, or transmitted in any form by any means—electronic, mechanical, photocopy, recording, or otherwise—without prior written permission of the author, except for the use of brief quotations in a book review and as provided by United States of America's copyright law. For permission requests, please refer all questions to the author: TonyWarrick.com.

Scripture quotations, unless otherwise noted, are taken from The ESV® Bible (The Holy Bible, English Standard Version®) copyright © 2001 by Crossway Bibles, a publishing ministry of Good News Publishers. ESV Text Edition: 2016. The ESV® text has been reproduced in cooperation with and by the permission of Good News Publishers. Unauthorized reproduction of this publication is prohibited. All rights reserved.

Cover design by Jamar Jones, www.gi-designs.com
Editorial services by Nyesha Sherman, Maryanne Dingman, and Ashley Warrick

Printed in the United States of America

ISBN: 978-1-955253-02-4

| Before We Get Started

Before we get started, if something is troubling your heart and robbing you of your peace of mind, I urge you to allow me and my team to pray for you. Send me a prayer request so my team and I can join you in prayer: tonywarrick.com/prayerrequest/

Also, don't forget to subscribe to my website and catch all my new releases, daily devotionals, and monthly newsletter. You can sign up here: tonywarrick.com

Contents

| Introduction 10

| Author's Note 20

1 | Christ Giving Light 24

2 | Leave Fear Behind 26

3 | Leapfrog Anxiety 28

4 | When Facing Challenges 30

5 | Rest in Who God Is 32

6 | Jesus Is With You 34

7 | Trust in the Lord 36

8 | Prayer: Disappointments of Life 38

9 | Renewed Strength 40

10 | God's Greatness 42

11 | Let Peace Rule 44

12 | Faith Walking 46

13 | Abundant Love 48

14 | Embrace Forgiveness 50

15 | Beyond Disappointment 52

16 | Prayer: Disappointed Heart 54

17 | Give It to Jesus 56

18 | God's Love Never Fails 58

19 | Prepare for Great Things 60

20 | Your Yes Activates God's Miracles 62

21 | Stretch Before the Blessing 64

22 | God's Higher Way 67

23 | Celebrate! 70

24 | God Approves You 74

25 | Kingdom-driven Life 76

26 | Jesus, the Best Decision 78

27 | Foundation of Wisdom 80

28 | Have Confidence in God 82

29 | When-Then Mindset 84

| 30 | The Unexpected 86
| 31 | Let God Be Big..88
| 32 | Prayer: The Path of Life 90
| 33 | A Reminder to Trust...92
| 34 | Watch Your Mouth 94
| 35 | Watch Your Focus 96
| 36 | Leave the Past Behind.......................................98
| 37 | We Serve A Limitless God 100
| 38 | Child of the Most-High God 102
| 39 | Original Masterpiece 104
| 40 | Certain Truths 106
| 41 | Be Blessed Abundantly...................................108
| 42 | When Facing Opposition 110
| 43 | Prayer: Save Me...112
| 44 | Is God Waiting On You? 114
| 45 | Obedience: Is It Worth It? 116

46 | Prayer: Obedient Heart 118

47 | Done Decently and In Order 120

48 | Change Your Attitude 122

49 | The Lord is Our Helper 126

50 | Delightfully Made 128

51 | Rest in the Work of Jesus 130

52 | Victory Is Our Heritage 132

53 | Realizing You Matter 134

54 | What You Do Matters 136

55 | It Does Not Matter 138

56 | Prayer: God My Protector 140

57 | In Due Season 142

58 | God Must Come First 144

59 | Don't Settle for Less 146

60 | Poised for a Resurrection 148

61 | The Same Holy Spirit 150

62 | The Golden Rule 152

63 | Keep Taking Steps..154

64 | Do Not Hold Back..156

65 | Receiving Your Blessing.................................158

66 | Faith and Patience 160

67 | Prayer: Patience..162

68 | Be A History Maker 164

69 | You Can Do It..166

70 | Give Me Strength 168

| Can You Do Me A Favor? 170

| About the Author 171

| Introduction

I'm going to confess; I think I may be addicted to Post-it Notes!

I leave them all over the place. I have them on my computer, in books, on the refrigerator, on my nightstand, in my gym bag; you can pretty much follow the trail of Post-it Notes to find me anywhere.

Okay… I admit, it's not just Post-it Notes that I'll write on. I scribble on anything I can get my hands on to leave myself a note.

Notes have become essential in my home. Perhaps, more significant than bread or milk. I write little notes to myself about everything. These notes are reminders, declarations, affirmations, nuggets of wisdom, and insights, written to help me get through the day.

Writing notes to myself reminds me of what is essential, what I think is significant, and what matters the most to me in my life. These notes have become my creative reference point that I can take action from, refer back to, and build into ideas. These notes help me improve my time management and increase my focus and productivity.

More Than A Note

I couldn't sleep many nights in college because my mind was always racing. I would find myself lying down in my bed, attempting to go to sleep, and my mind would begin to wander, pursuing different ideas and concepts. Words and sentences would start formulating, transferring thoughts and philosophies to my heart.

Can I be candid with you for a moment? It felt like another person had taken control of my mind, making me question the meaning of life, challenging my understanding of the world. It felt like someone took over my hand's function, and I would write little notes, opening the floodgates of my emotions. Years later, I realized that person was the Lord, downloading ideas, notions, questions, and concepts through the Holy Spirit to help me become a better person, to help me become Christ-like.

I have collected countless notes of godly wisdom, inspiration, and insights from the Word of God and other Holy Spirit-inspired writings. These notes have encouraged me to live life with positivity, gratitude, and grace. These godly insights have helped me understand that I was not a victim of my circumstances but a victor, overcoming my circumstances.

One day, I began to feel a sense of responsibility, an obligation, to express the thoughts flowing through my mind in an organized way. Therefore, I started to look for a realistic way to record my ideas and opinions, so I began journaling.

In the beginning, journaling was great. It provided me the opportunity to learn new lessons from old experiences. It motivated me to make the most of each day while providing me with proof of my progress. However, I quickly learned that journaling wasn't enough for me.

I started to feel the weight of my thoughts, a burden to take my notes and publicize them to the world. So, in 2006, I started writing most of my insights on Facebook to release the heaviness I was feeling from this burden. To tell you the truth, when I first started posting on Facebook, my only purpose was to remove the weight I was feeling. My approach was simple; express what I was feeling and thinking.

I didn't care if anyone was reading my post or not. I didn't care if people agreed with the post or not. I didn't care if people felt offended or not. I wasn't hoping someone would click the like button to validate what I was saying. And if I'm going to be completely honest with you, a large part of me still don't care. All I wanted to do was healthily express my thoughts. However, about five months later, something interesting happened.

I was attending my college's homecoming celebration when a fraternity brother came up to me and said,

"Tony, your messages on Facebook have been helping me. Please keep posting your quotes. You are probably helping a lot of people. People who struggle to articulate how they are feeling. People who you will probably never meet."

The words of my frat brother moved me. So, that is precisely what I did! I kept posting all my ideas, notions, and concepts on Facebook to serve others so that God may be glorified.

When I started sharing my insights on different social media platforms, I was amazed at how they resonated with people worldwide. I was astonished by the impact it was having on people's lives. Readers from all over the world would write to me, sharing their stories about how my words helped them daily. They shared how they used my social media messages to help them make critical decisions and provide a level of encouragement.

I felt, and still feel, truly blessed that God is using me as a vessel to provide impactful messages. The Lord has, and still is, connecting me with some fantastic individuals who are on the same path as I am, seeking God's truths to advance His Kingdom. Therefore, I must say, with a joyful heart, I give God all the glory for using me to provide individuals with a level of soul care!

What is Soul Care?

Soul Care is the ongoing work of nourishing and nurturing one's soul. It is fundamentally learning to live our lives with God. Soul care is not about what we are doing; it's about what God is doing in us and through us. We simply place ourselves in a position for God to care for us and attend to our souls. Nevertheless, to properly nourish and care for our souls, we need to understand what the soul is.

There are many words for "soul" in ancient Hebrew, but the most commonly used words are *"nefesh"* and *"neshamah"*—both of which mean "the breath." The two words are found together in Genesis 2:7, which recounts how the first human (Adam) received the breath of life (neshamah) from God and became a living soul (nefesh ḥayyah).

"...then the Lord God formed the man of dust from the ground and breathed into his nostrils the breath of life, and the man became a living creature" Genesis 2:7

The soul is one of three dimensions of the human experience: body, soul, and spirit. Similar to the human experience, the soul also has three dimensions: Ruach, Neshamah, and Chayah.

1. Ruach is one's moral and emotional self; spiritedness.
2. Neshama is one's intellectual self; comprehension.
3. Chayah is one's supra-rational self; the seat of will, desire, commitment, and faith.

In other words, the soul is one's emotions, mind, and will.

Let's dig deeper for a more in-depth understanding of the soul by looking at a different passage of scripture.

Then God said, "Let us make man in our image, after our likeness. And let them have dominion over the fish of the sea and over the birds of the heavens and over the livestock and over all the earth and over every creeping thing that creeps on the earth." So God created man in his own image, in the image of God he created him; male and female he created them. Genesis 1:26-27

The statement, ***"So God created man in His own image,"*** does not refer to looking alike but being alike. The intent of God was to express His soulful nature through humanity. Our soulful God created humans as soulful beings. Human beings were created to be communicated through one's spirit, and that communication is manifested through one's soul (mind, emotions, and will), eventually finding expression through one's physical body. So, let me wrap up all this information by saying,

You are not a body with a spirit and a soul; rather, you are a spirit with a soul living on the earth inside a body.

In other words, within you is a soul, and nothing happens in the soul that is not reflected in the body. And nothing happens in the body that doesn't profoundly affect the soul. A slight deficiency in the body is a significant deficiency in the soul. The opposite is true as well; if there is a problem in the body, its origin is somewhere in the soul. The two must be healed in tandem. Heal the body by healing the soul — with more love, kindness, prayer, and forgiveness. Allow your body to flourish and prosper by taking care of your soul.

So, what is soul care?

Soul care is the ongoing work of nourishing and nurturing one's mind, will, and emotion. God created human beings to live from the inside out, speaking the truth in love while depending on the authority and rule of the Lord.

There is no doubt that a healthy soul (our mind, will, and emotions) is vital to winning in life. Many individuals with extraordinary spiritual gifts and even excellent physical health have had their destinies sabotaged because they have never learned to manage their emotions, willpower, or mentalities. Soul weakness is an Achilles heel that eventually takes them out of their race.

The Heart of the Matter

God loves you, and He cares about who you are becoming. Therefore, it's vital that we care for our souls (our mind, will, and emotions), positioning ourselves in such a way as to allow God's Spirit to form us in the likeness of Christ, God's Anointed One.

This book, Soul Care, is an extension of my messages from social media. Within these pages, you will find notes I have written to myself, which will help you have a healthy soul so that God may be glorified in all things. You will feel empowered through the book's use of prayers and scriptures, soul-searching insights, simplicity, and affirmations.

The core of it all, the primary purpose of this book, is to help you. More importantly, it is to help your emotions, your will, and your mind connect with the wisdom of God, so you can make a great commitment to a great cause while overcoming great challenges to achieve great success and great significance.

I hope this book becomes a seed to help you discover how:

- to be more connected to the Lord,
- to be more in harmony with yourself and others,
- to be more thoughtful with your relationships,
- to be more involved with your community,
- and to be more conscious of your world.

This book is designed to be carried with you so you can read messages when you need motivation, inspiration, and encouragement. Therefore, you can put this book on your coffee table. Keep it in your office. Or on the nightstand beside your bed. You can become who God created you to become and do what God has called you to do with a little soul care.

Beloved, I pray that all may go well with you and that you may be in good health, as it goes well with your soul. ~ **3 John 1:2**

| Author's Note

"As a deer pants for flowing streams, so pants my soul for you, O God. My soul thirsts for God, for the living God…" **Psalm 42:1-2**

During these days of uncertainty and unrest, it's essential to start and end our days by replenishing our souls. Just like our physical bodies need to be fed every day to stay healthy, so do our souls. If we are not feeding our souls, we're going to feel emotionally and spiritually drained.

It is not enough to empty our minds of negative thoughts, views, and opinions. We must go a step further and fill it with God's truths. Our thoughts and our words are an expression of our lives. We must think godly and affirm godly ideas to enrich a godly experience and a godly life.

This book was written as a tool to feed your soul. It was written to be used as a form of advice. Soul Care was written to awaken the unspeakable joy, unconditional love, and the peace of God at your command.

Therefore, if you need guidance from the Holy Spirit, ask Him: *What do I need to know right now?* Then, think of a number between 1 and 70, and look up the insight attached to your chosen number. Since the number you pick will be based on your thought, the insights will become meaningful while connecting you to the Word of God.

All the insights in this book have one purpose, to help heighten your awareness of a loving heavenly Father by reminding you of who He is and who you are. And as you discover more of who God is and what He says in this book, your thoughts will start to reflect His thoughts, and you will start becoming more Christ-like.

Part 1: Soul Care…
CONNECT TO GOD

GOD CANNOT RULE YOUR LIFE IF EMOTIONS RULE YOUR LIFE!

1 | Christ Giving Light

For at one time you were darkness, but now you are light in the Lord. Walk as children of light. **Ephesians 5:8**

Why do we need light? It is because light tells us the place of each thing through our physical and spiritual eyes. It is because, in truth, each thing has a place, and in that place, it is good (because God is good) regardless if we think so or not. In other words, light doesn't add anything or take away. It only reveals the meaning of all that it shines upon.

Light and darkness cannot coexist; darkness is dissipated because light is always stronger whenever light encounters darkness. Therefore, we do not need to fear a dark world; instead, we must go into that world and release the light of Christ through hope, grace, mercy, love, justice, and truth. We must shine our light and heal the world.

The shining light of Christ is intended to not only guide our path but to help those around us find a way through their darkness and point them toward the life God has waiting for them. As long as our light is absent, the world will remain to be dark.

Note to Self

Dear Self,

Hiding your hurt only deepens the pain, and problems grow in the dark. But if you expose your pain, frustration, and anger to Christ's light and truth, your hurt will begin to shrink. The light of Jesus will give you peace. The Lord's light will allow you to become a light for the world.

Jesus said, ***"Let your light shine before others" (Matthew 5:16a).*** He explained that no one lights a lamp to hide it under a basket. A lamp is meant to be placed on a stand to give light to everything around it. Therefore, no matter how successful or unsuccessful you become, you must always seek to be a shining example of Jesus's light and love, a beacon of hope for people.

Focus on letting the Holy Spirit be your guide this week. Go to Him for your next step and watch Him pave the way before you with goodness and mercy. Christ is the Lord of wholeness and healing, so do not be afraid to ask Him for strength to be the light. Now go, and let God's words guide you. Let your light shine and bring glory to Him.

With Love,

Self

2 | Leave Fear Behind

I sought the Lord, and he answered me and delivered me from all my fears. **Psalm 34:4**

- The fear of failure is worse than failure.
- The fear of rejection is worse than rejection.
- The fear of not fitting in is worse than not fitting in.

Why? It is because the emotion of fear is felt as a sense of dread, alerting us to the possibility that we might be harmed, which motivates us to protect ourselves. Nonetheless, fear is the false evidence appearing real. It is the misunderstanding of the past, misinterpretation of current events, and the unpredictability of the future.

Did you know God never intended for us to settle for a life of living uninspired, confined to safe daily routines? Instead, He created us on purpose for a purpose, and He wants us to venture out in faith. In other words, we cannot let fear stop us from being who God destined us to be. Therefore, when fear comes knocking at our emotional door, we must answer it with faith.

Note to Self

Dear Self,

Don't let your fear hold you back today. There are so many things God wants to do through you, and as you step out in faith, He will order your steps and take care of the rest!

Here are two ways to confront your fear:

1. **Practice being in the presence of God.**

    You must begin with worship! Celebrate the power and faithfulness of God. When you become mindful of God's presence in your life, fear will go away.

2. **Move against fear with faith.**

    You cannot go around fear, nor can you go over or under it. You must tackle fear by going through it with faith and by faith. Therefore, meditate on what God says about you; you will be able to recognize the fears in your life as false evidence appearing real.

Remember, you are gifted! You are smart! And God has qualified you! With Jesus on your side, there is nothing to fear!

With Love,

Self

3 | Leapfrog Anxiety

Do not be anxious about anything, but in everything by prayer and supplication with thanksgiving let your requests be made known to God. And the peace of God, which surpasses all understanding, will guard your hearts and your minds in Christ Jesus. **Philippians 4:6-7**

Stress, worry, fear, all of those emotions can rise up within us and leave us screaming on the inside; I'm anxious! But there is the good news: You can overcome the feeling of anxiousness.

Think of anxiety as long-term fear. It can lie to us and make us feel insignificant. It builds stress within our souls. It lures us into believing there are no answers. It's typically focused on the future rather than the present.

Please understand anxiety is not from the Lord, and it is not more powerful than our God. He knew that anxiety would come to steal our peace and harmony. So, in His boundless compassion and faithfulness to us, God made a way for us to be more than equipped to overcome its effects.

If we pray with a thankful heart, the peace of God will guard our hearts and souls while helping us leapfrog over our anxieties and fears.

Note to Self

Dear Self,

Are you allowing anxiety to become an obstacle between you and your destiny? Whenever anxiety tries to grip you, the enemy will try to take you down and frighten you out of trusting the Lord. But the meaningless games the Devil play is no match for the Holy Spirit who lives inside of you, nor for the faith, love, and hope the Father has given you.

You need to depend on, draw on, and walk with peace because the Holy Spirit in you is greater than anything or anyone that comes against you.

With Love,

Self

SELF-REFLECTIONS

Think of something you've been worrying about. What is an action step you can take instead of worrying?

_____

_____

_____

_____

_____

4 | When Facing Challenges

Count it all joy, my brothers, when you meet trials of various kinds, for you know that the testing of your faith produces steadfastness. And let steadfastness have its full effect, that you may be perfect and complete, lacking in nothing. **James 1:2-4**

Many times, we tend to view the hardships of life as attacks from the adversary. However, just as Abraham, the father of our faith, was tested, we, the spiritual children of Abraham, should also expect testing, and we should learn to embrace it. The fact is that tests are not for God, but they are for us. When we pass our tests and overcome our challenges, our faith in God is demonstrated to the world. And sometimes, passing that test and overcoming our difficulties let us know that we are capable of even more than we realize.

Note to Self

Dear Self,

Trials and tribulations do not mean you are out of the will of God. Trials frequently suggest you are doing precisely what you are supposed to be doing, fighting the good fight of faith. Therefore, stand firm and keep believing because God is working all things for your good.

God's love, which is known to you and claimed you before you were even born, can take you beyond yourself. His love can bring you through emotional earthquakes. His love can lift you out of betrayal and hurt. It can deliver you from any heartache. When all else is shaken and fails, His love never fails, and it is unmovable.

I know it will take bravery to keep believing and moving forward, especially when your present circumstances look nothing like you expected. But, that is when you have to hold onto God's promises in faith and by faith, and move forward with power and authority.

It is time for you to press in and press on and not let fear cause you to give up too soon. Do not waiver in your faith! Do not give up in the middle of a test! God is preparing something extraordinary for everything you have been through.

Your time of increase is coming! You will succeed and prosper! God is with you when you are facing challenges!
With Love,
Self

5 | Rest in Who God Is

He who dwells in the shelter of the Most-High will abide in the shadow of the Almighty. **Psalm 91:1**

When you feel like everything is falling apart, don't give up. When things aren't working out like you planned or anticipated, don't give up. When people let you down or hurt your feelings, don't give up!

We need to remember nothing can keep us away from experiencing what God has for us. The enemy would love for us to think we have gone too far or messed up too severely. But Jesus took every bit of our sins upon Himself. What we have done in the past does not change who God is. If we surrender ourselves to God's purpose and rest in who God is, we will experience a life of adventure, passion, and joy.

We all have a habit of trusting things like dependable friends and financial stability, but these temporary comforts can never serve as our sufficient refuge or foundation. God is our exclusive refuge when times are good and when the world we live in falls apart. In other words, the assurance of God's help is our hope, even if the mountain crumbles into the sea because He is the one who spoke everything into existence.

Note to Self

Dear Self,

When you rest in who God is, nothing can sway you! That's the beauty of having yourself planted in faith; extreme feelings of doubt and fear are quickly shut down because you know that God is in control. Therefore, during life's storms, always remember that God is full of grace, love, mercy, forgiveness, redemption, healing, and peace.

Keep your focus on the Lord, not the obstacles, hurdles, disappointments, or circumstances in your way. Place what you do know about the Lord above what you don't know about the future or what you might not understand about people. As you do this, I know you're going to experience His presence like you never have before.

Just keep doing what the Lord has told you to do because ultimately, God goes before you, protects you, favors you, and you can rest in who God is. Here is a quote to remember: **Peace is not just the absence of a storm but rest in the middle of the storm.**

With Love,

Self

6 | No Matter What Happens, Jesus Is With You

The Lord is my shepherd; I shall not want. He makes me lie down in green pastures. He leads me beside still waters. He restores my soul. He leads me in paths of righteousness for his name's sake. **Psalm 23:1-3**

Are you ready to increase your faith today? Because, while there may be an enemy against us, we have an overcoming King who is with us, who is for us, and who will never leave us or forsake us.

The Lord is with us wherever we go. He promises to be a lamp for our feet. If we live by faith and not by sight, we are promised everything will be all right, working according to the will of God.

I know the feeling of being completely alone is a real issue. So many of us have had to wrestle through it, perhaps now more than ever! The human experience leaves us vulnerable to emotions that tell us no one understands us, nobody has been through what we are going through, or at the very least, there isn't anyone who cares. And as life continues, betrayal, abuse, abandonment, trauma, and many other things leave us damaged with insecurity, isolation, and loneliness. But, when life seems out of control and lonely, we can be sure of this, Jesus is with us.

Note to Self

Dear Self,

If you ever fear the present, all you need to do is look back and see how God took care of you in the past. People may do you wrong, but Jesus will be your defender because He is your king. Situations may look impossible, but the impossible is possible with the Lord.

Therefore, be strong and courageous in the Lord. Don't give up on Him. Don't stop believing in Him. Don't walk away from His plans and purposes for your life.

Walk with confidence because Jesus' mercies, love, and grace will never end; they are new every morning. And when you least expect it, by faith, doors will open, and by faith, your breakthrough will come. You will abide in and be abandoned in Jesus' sovereignty and faithfulness!

With Love,

Self

7 | Trust in the Lord

Commit your way to the Lord; trust in him, and he will act. **Psalm 37:5**

When the nation of Israel left Egypt headed towards the Promised Land, God led them the long way around. That's right; God led them into a hard wilderness season of life. There was a shortcut, but God didn't show them that way. How often in our own lives does God lead us the long way around?

There is always a wilderness between where you are and where you're going. We need to embrace the long way around and trust that God is using that time to prepare us for what He has already prepared for us.

Note to Self

Dear Self,

I have one word for you today: **COMMITMENT!**

Never stop growing closer to the Lord. Remain committed to pursuing all He has for you, going from faith to faith, from glory to glory, and from increase to increase regardless of what is happening around you.

Understand, life is a journey of faith, and within that journey, there will be detours, but Jesus is your shepherd, moving you closer to your destination. His will for you is for you to live a victorious life overflowing with success. But He doesn't promise to leave it at your doorstep. You have a significant role to play, and that role will involve you taking some risks.

To live a life of victory and pursue your divine assignments with everything you have, you will have to leave your comfort zone and enter the unknown. You have to believe the best about God and cultivate your hope in Him. You have to learn to trust God and be open to seeing things from a new perspective. You have to know that all things work together for your good. Your test will be your testimony.

Rest in that promise today and receive everything the Lord has for you.

With Love,

Self

8 | Prayer: Trust for The Disappointments of Life

Heavenly Father,

Your name is great and powerful among all the nations! You set Your splendor and glory above the heavens. Out of the mouths of Your beloved, You established power to silence the adversary.

Loving God, I humbly come before you because there are times when difficulties and disappointments come my way, and it's too much to endure. I find myself stressing out and worrying about everything that is happening in my life. I know this is not how the Christian life should be lived, but if I am honest, I don't understand how to live a satisfying life unto You, even though I have tried so very hard.

Lord, I ask for Your help to develop a new level of trust in every area of my life. I want to trust You now, so help me cast all my burdens on You. Help me not to be moved by my feelings but to make Your Word my final authority. When the disappointments in my life seem to be piling up all around me, help me trust You with all my heart and soul, and not lean on my own understanding or rely on myself.

Help me to seek You and Your Kingdom first, knowing that all the other things will be added unto me. Help me to trust You instead of trusting in myself. I want to develop unwavering hope and rest in You. I want to grow in my understanding of Your character, so I may know You better.

Lord, I choose to run to You, to trust You, and refuse to get into disappointment. You are worthy of my faith and love. I will trust You with my salvation and with my daily life.

In Jesus' name. Amen

9 | Renewed Strength

Have you not known? Have you not heard? The Lord is the everlasting God, the Creator of the ends of the earth. He does not faint or grow weary; his understanding is unsearchable. He gives power to the faint, and to him who has no might he increases strength. Even youths shall faint and be weary, and young men shall fall exhausted; but they who wait for the Lord shall renew their strength; they shall mount up with wings like eagles; they shall run and not be weary; they shall walk and not faint.

Isaiah 40:28-31

In your weariness and despair, have you ever wondered: Can God's promise really be true? Let us remember this quote:

People grow weary. But the Lord does not. And those who hope in Him will find their strength renewed.

God is above all; He is not like us. He does not grow weary as we do. His understanding of His creation, His authority, and His purpose is beyond our ability to comprehend. We may feel abandoned, left to our own devices. Nevertheless, be assured, the Lord has not forgotten us. We may not understand what He is doing. But we can rest assured that He is in control and in charge.

Note to Self

Dear Self,

Do you find yourself tired? Are you worn out? Feeling weighed down with everything you're trying to accomplish? I know it is tempting to give up on your dreams because, at times, you have grown weary with the preparation. However, you must remember good things come to those who wait on the Lord, but God's best comes to those preparing while they are waiting.

It may be time to take an inventory of your ambitions and motivations. When you are running your race from a place of godly purpose, the Lord is faithful to give you the renewed strength and energy you need to run well. Stay the course and inherit the promises of God! The Lord invites you to come to Him and find hope and strength.

With Love,

Self

10 | God's Greatness

For the Lord God is a sun and shield; the Lord bestows favor and honor. No good thing does he withhold from those who walk uprightly.
Psalm 84:11

What are the things that keep you from moving forward in faith and by faith? What is keeping you from experiencing God's very best? What are your what-ifs:

- What if my friends reject me?
- What if I apply, and I'm not chosen?
- What if I write a book and no one buys it?
- What if I try and it doesn't work?

Throughout my life, I've realized that fear is the greatest killer of purpose and destiny. The question of "What if?" can paralyze and cripple people to the point of never moving forward. Nonetheless, we have to make God bigger than our what-ifs. We should not focus on the mountain that is in front of us. We need to focus on God, who can move the mountain. We need to focus on God's greatness!

It is not hard to discover the depths of God's feelings for us. When the enemy creates a web to entangle us, God's love and promises break its stronghold and place us in an atmosphere of blessings and favor so that we can become everything He created us to become.

Note to Self

Dear Self,

Look around you and see how vast this universe is, which God has made. Numerous galaxies, beautiful stars, unique planets, fantastic mountain ranges, and life-sustaining rivers and oceans; your God is indeed an all-powerful God.

The greatness of God's power is beyond your imagination and comprehension. He is committed to and is more than able to fulfill His promises to those who have faith in Him. Therefore, as you grow into a profound place of passion and intimate love with the Father, you will become confident in the truth that as long as God is with you, nothing can work against you. God turns all oppositions around for your greatest good.

So, today, become occupied with the Lord's greatness instead of your smallness. If you walk along His paths with integrity, you will never lack anything you need.

With Love,

Self

11 | Let Peace Rule

Do not be anxious about anything, but in every situation, by prayer and petition, with thanksgiving, present your requests to God. And the peace of God, which transcends all understanding, will guard your hearts and your minds in Christ Jesus. **Philippians 4:6-7**

Peace is a critical attribute of our faith. In the Land of Israel, the Priest, the descendants of Aaron, bless the people with peace every day. In Psalms, we are told to request and pursue peace. In Proverbs, it tells us that all the paths of the Word of God lead to peace.

The world defines "peace" as freedom from disturbance, and it is synonymous with compromise. However, in ancient Hebrew, the word for peace is *"shalom,"* from the root *shalem*, which means "wholeness." In the language of the Bible, if there is wholeness, then there is peace. The two go together. We do not achieve peace through division, fragmentation, or freedom from trouble but instead through completeness.

When we are in peace, we are in a position of power. Peace is not the absence of trouble. Peace is knowing God is right there with us in the midst of the trouble because we are made whole through Christ.

<u>Note to Self</u>

Dear Self,

You will all go through moments and seasons that feel unbearable and confusing. But the truth you can hold on to is that the Lord will never leave your side. He is with you, and even when what you're asking for doesn't come to pass, He will still hold you in His presence and fill your soul with unwavering peace.

You must allow God's peace to rule in your heart! To be honest, you cannot be at peace with others unless you are at peace. Therefore, do not focus your thoughts on what may cause you to worry or be anxious. Choose to go to God and give Him what you are feeling burdened by. As you do this, His peace is going to reign in your heart!

With Love,

Self

12 | Faith Walking

For by grace you have been saved through faith. And this is not your own doing; it is the gift of God, not a result of works, so that no one may boast. **Ephesians 2:8-9**

Did you know that our faith can bind up the brokenhearted and declare liberty to those family members feeling captive? Our faith can proclaim the favor of the Lord and can bring comfort to all who mourn. Because of our faith, our families will be called righteous, and Jesus will be glorified.

Genuine faith isn't about what we see or feel. Faith is about God, who He is, what He's done, and what He's promised us in His Word. And it's His Word that provides the light we need to guide us through each day, even when life is complicated.

As we remain faithful to follow and obey the Lord, He will bring our families and us into a place of pleasure and fulfillment. God is not asking us to walk by sight; He is asking us to walk by faith. He is asking us to trust Him because His plans are always for our good. We have power and authority; therefore, we should speak faith over ourselves, our family, finances, and dreams! Our greatness is coming by faith and through faith!

Note to Self

Dear Self,

It is the Lord's will that you would live an overflowing, purpose-filled, fruitful life. He has already declared His promises for you. The Lord is waiting for you to step out in faith to take hold of them.

Often, stepping out involves great courage, it requires you to take some risks, and God's directions may not even make sense to you. Nonetheless, take risks anyway because it is an opportunity for your faith to grow.

Get up every day and focus on your faith in God through Jesus Christ and how you can be a blessing, and not how you can get blessed. Understand, the Lord will meet your needs as well as your family's needs. In due season, you will reap a harvest of blessings and an increase of faith.

With Love,

Self

13 | Abundant Love

"You shall love the Lord your God with all your heart and with all your soul and with all your strength and with all your mind, and your neighbor as yourself." **Luke 10:27**

You know the question. It is the ultimate question. The question that everyone has laid awake at night thinking about. The question that brings equal parts wonder and terror to our delicate minds. The question is:

What is the meaning of life?

To understand the meaning of our lives, we have to begin with God's nature. God is love. Love is the essence of His nature. In fact, the only reason there is love in the world is because of God.

So, what is the meaning of life? The true meaning of life is to LOVE!

The Bible says love is a command (2 John 1:6). The Bible says love is a choice (1 Corinthians 14:1). The Bible says love is a behavior (1 John 3:18). The Bible says love is an obligation (1 John 4:16).

Love bears all things, believes all things, hopes all things, endures all things. This is why we must first love God with all our hearts, with all our souls, and with all our minds. We must love our neighbors as ourselves.

Note to Self

Dear Self,

Of all your life's experiences, nothing engages you, moves you, shakes you, reaches deep inside you, molds you, and expresses for you, like love.

Love is the golden law for the Kingdom of God. It is the heart of the gospel. As a follower of Jesus, you are called to bring peace where there is chaos, kindness where there is hurt, and love, unconditional love, where there is judgment and hatred. You are called to learn to live a life marked by peace, kindness, and LOVE.

Therefore, if you want to wake up and feel empowered, you must passionately fall in love with JOY – Jesus, Others, and Yourself. And never forget: ***"For God so loved the world, that he gave his only Son, that whoever believes in him should not perish but have eternal life" (John 3:16).***

With Love,

Self

14 | Embrace Forgiveness

If we confess our sins, he is faithful and just to forgive us our sins and to cleanse us from all unrighteousness. **1 John 1:9**

Sometimes the most challenging person for us to forgive is the individual we see in the mirror. And if we are honest with ourselves, there are times when we are so upset with ourselves for past failures and choices that we struggle to move forward to achieve our dreams. We try to embrace our moments of greatness, but we struggle because we feel ashamed and guilty.

Nevertheless, we have to realize the way we feel about ourselves is not how God thinks or feels about us. Instead of giving us the punishment we deserve, Jesus Christ paid for all our sins and all our wrongs. In fact, refusing to forgive ourselves for what God has already forgiven insults King Jesus. It implies that what He did on the cross wasn't enough for us.

Quote to Remember

Self-forgiveness is key to unlocking genuine relationships.

Note to Self

Dear Self,

Forgiving yourself begins with embracing the truth that your heavenly Father has forgiven you. Starting today, decide to forgive yourself for all the cruel, heartless, and nasty things you have thought about yourself, and never forget that you are God's masterpiece!

With Love,

Self

SELF-REFLECTIONS

How can God's grace and forgiveness affect your view of yourself?

_____

_____

_____

_____

_____

_____

_____

_____

_____

15 | Beyond Disappointment

Blessed be the God and Father of our Lord Jesus Christ, the Father of mercies and God of all comfort, who comforts us in all our affliction, so that we may be able to comfort those who are in any affliction, with the comfort with which we ourselves are comforted by God.
2 Corinthians 1:3-4

We were each fashioned to run a race unique to us and to pass our faith to the next generation as we go. Nonetheless, as we run, the enemy shouts at us from the sidelines, trying to confuse us. He would love nothing more than for us to swerve off course or stop running because of our disappointments.

All the disappointment in the world will never change God's promises or His purpose for our lives. The disappointments are real and the consequences can be devastating. However, none of our disappointments can stop His desire for us to fulfill our purposes.

To keep moving forward, we must learn to manage our disappointments well. We must learn to be resilient. We must learn to be patient in tribulation, be constant in prayer, so we can keep moving forward full of renewed hope.

Note to Self

Dear Self,

God is inviting you to make more room for Him in your heart. He wants to do great work in you so that He can do great work through you. However, your heart is filled with disappointments, taking up too much space and crowding God out. Let go of the disappointments and watch the Lord bless you beyond comprehension. Remember these three things:

1. God can use your disappointments to set a new path for you.

2. There are divine appointments beyond all your disappointments. Therefore, cast all your anxieties, concerns, and doubts on the Lord because He cares about you.

3. God using your disappointments for good certainly doesn't take the disappointments away, but it will give you peace and contentment.

You are never alone. God will never forsake you. And He will lead you through the valley toward the mountaintop of victory He already has for you!

With Love,

Self

16 | Prayer: Disappointed Heart

Heavenly Father,

I come before You, Lord, with a heart weighed down by disappointments. Life has not turned out as I expected; and at times, I feel like a failure. I feel like my life is a disaster. Part of me wants to complain, part of me wants to give up in hopelessness, and part of me wonders why I keep trying.

Even though I feel this way, I choose to believe Your words. You are mighty to deliver. Because of Your mighty hand, You will drive out the forces that have set themselves up against me. Your magnificent Spirit reminds me that Your strength is made perfect in my weakness, and You have fashioned everything to work together in perfect harmony.

Father, forgive me for complaining about my issues. Forgive me for wallowing in my self-pity. Forgive me for my discontentment. Please help me to access the power to look beyond the disappointments of now.

It is You who will bring me out from under the yoke of bondage and free me from being a slave to disappointments. I need You to flood my heart with Your strength and redeem me with an outstretched arm, with mighty acts of love.

With patience and active persistence, I run the race, the appointed course set before me. I rebuke the spirit of fear, for I am established in righteousness. Oppression and destruction shall not come near me. I am more than a conqueror through Him who loves me.

It is in Jesus' name, I pray, Amen.

17 | Give It to Jesus

"And taking the five loaves and the two fish, he looked up to heaven and said a blessing over them. Then he broke the loaves and gave them to the disciples to set before the crowd. And they all ate and were satisfied. And what was left over was picked up, twelve baskets of broken pieces." **Luke 9:16-17**

It is astonishing to read how Jesus blessed something that was not enough and made it plenty. What seemed like little became so much more in the hands of Jesus.

Amazing things can happen when we give what we have into the hands of a miracle-working Lord!

Note to Self

Dear Self,

The Lord came up with the idea of multiplication. Let me explain:

If you give Jesus your time, He multiplies it. If you give Jesus your money, He multiplies it. If you give Jesus your talent, He multiplies it. If you give Jesus your energy, guess what? He multiplies it! It's the same principle as planting seeds. 2 Corinthians 9:10 says, **"He who supplies seed to the sower and bread for food will supply and multiply**

your seed for sowing and increase the harvest of your righteousness."

Therefore, start giving God thanks for what He has done in the past. Until you can be thankful for what is not enough, you will not be able to provide the Lord with the room to operate and multiply what you have into more than enough. You must give Him authority over everything you own, including your life.

Lastly, even if you do not see the Lord working now, trust Him to do what He promised. I believe God wants to take the little you feel you can offer Him today and multiply it into something so much more than you could ever imagine. Your gratitude and love will release multiplication!

With Love,

Self

Additional Scripture:

Jesus then took the loaves, and when he had given thanks, he distributed them to those who were seated. So also the fish, as much as they wanted. And when they had eaten their fill, he told his disciples, "Gather up the leftover fragments, that nothing may be lost." **John 6:11-12**

18 | God's Love Never Fails

And above all these put on love, which binds everything together in perfect harmony. **Colossians 3:14**

While God is always calling us forward, we can feel imprisoned by the mistakes of our past. Whether it's abuse, addiction, regret, shame, guilt, lust, condemnation, apathy, indifference, or greed — we lock ourselves up within our wrongdoings. But at some point, we have to ask ourselves, "Why are we stuck, feeling imprisoned?"

When we genuinely get the revelation that God's love never fails, that He forgives, and that He has a destiny for us, it frees us from our past!

Love is God, and God is love. Everything God does is driven and influenced by His love. His love surpasses all human knowledge.

It is challenging for any of us to grasp the width, length, height, and depth of God's love. However, we need to know God does not love us because of our character; He loves us because of His perfect character.

Note to Self

Dear Self,

Are you ready to experience the incredible future God has for you?

God longs to have a loving relationship with you. His love goes beyond any human love you have ever experienced. If you decide to lean into the unconditional, unfailing, unbreakable love of the Father, your love will become patient, generous, unbiased, and forgiving. You will be able to overcome any betrayal, hurt, or crushing defeat. You will have an influence far more significant than you could ever envision, allowing you to step into an awesome future.

Therefore, live with the confidence that there is nothing in the universe with the power or authority to separate you from God's love. His love triumphs over death, life's troubles, and broken hearts. There is nothing in your present or future that can weaken His love. There is no power above you or beneath you—no power that can distance you from God's devoted unconditional love.

With Love,

Self

19 | Prepare for Great Things

For the Lord your God is he who goes with you to fight for you against your enemies, to give you the victory. **Deuteronomy 20:4**

David was anointed king of Israel when he was a teenager. However, it took 20 more years before he would be appointed to that position of king. During those 20 years, God prepared David for the calling He had prepared for him. And that's precisely how God works in our lives.

God puts dreams in our hearts and writes a purpose over our lives. And if we trust Him and take Him at His word, we will find ourselves on a path toward the fulfillment of those dreams. Unfortunately, the path that takes us to our dreams will be complex and challenging. God allows the path to be problematic because He intends on refining us and preparing us for our place of promise. In other words, He is not preparing the dreams for us; He is preparing us for the dreams so they can become a reality.

The prophet Isaiah encourages us, **"Arise, shine, for your light has come, and the glory of the LORD has risen upon you" (Isaiah 60:1).**

Note to Self

Dear Self,

The enemy of your soul would love for you to take cover under the weight of your struggles and disappointments, agreeing to a lifestyle of mediocrity and defeat. But you are made for so much more! Your heavenly Father has called you to great things.

God has a great assignment for you, and He will prepare you well in advance for what He has called you to do. Now, you may feel the pressure to promote or advance yourself. However, by understanding you are anointed, you will discover the discipline to wait in the season of preparation so you will be fully ready when God launches you into what He has called you to do. God is raising you up like a strong tower to shine brightly for the world to see!

Always remember, you were created to win! You were fashioned to overcome challenges. You were born to be a champion. Keep an attitude of faith because what seems impossible to accomplish is possible with Jesus in your life.

With Love,

Self

20 | Your Yes Activates God's Miracles

As for me, I would seek God, and to God would I commit my cause, who does great things and unsearchable, marvelous things without number: **Job 5:8-9**

What if Mary had said "no" to giving birth to Jesus? What would have happened if she had let fear rule her decisions instead of walking forward in faith? Thankfully, Mary had enough faith in the Lord to say "yes" and trust God with the rest. Her "yes" activated the miracle of the birth of the Savior of the world, the King of kings.

There are so many moments when God is trying to use us, but we are too scared or unsure to trust Him enough to pull us through it. And it's in these moments that we need to remember our God is faithful, and He will honor our obedience and faith.

Note to Self

Dear Self,

What fear is stopping you from walking confidently in your purpose? Is it fear of disappointment? Fear of what your friends or family might think or say? Fear of looking silly and foolish?

I'm here to tell you that if you're waiting not to feel afraid, you will never step out in faith and walk into your purpose and destiny. Furthermore, the Lord never asks, "Can you?" He simply asks, "Will you?"

If you want to impact your community for God's glory, you have to learn to live faith-full instead of fear-full so you can fulfill all that God has in store for you. God, in all of His greatness, can take care of any lack you may have. He will call you to achieve the impossible when you are living by faith and not by sight. By the grace of God, you will accomplish things you have never been able to do in the past!

When you have enough faith to say "yes" and continue saying "yes" to God, there's no limit to what He will do. Your "yes" can activate your miracle!

With Love,

Self

21 | Stretch Before the Blessing

The steadfast love of the Lord never ceases; his mercies never come to an end; they are new every morning; great is your faithfulness.
Lamentations 3:22-23

Sometimes, we cry out to God because we feel stuck in some area of our lives. We want to soar! We are ready to jump into our destiny. But just as it is in the art of dancing, stretching is vital to performing well consistently.

To stretch is to be made longer or wider without tearing or snapping. If we want to go from where we are to where God wants us to be, then we're going to need to stretch without breaking. Stretching will involve pain. It will include experiences we have never experienced before.

Stretching will involve inconveniences. It will involve setbacks. It will involve hard work. But the growth we want is in the stretch.

In everything that God will call us to do, God will lead us to be stretched. We must understand that we face significant increases and growth when stretched past doubts, uncertainties, and comfort. To do what God has called us to do, to be blessed, to achieve our dreams, we will have to be stretched.

Note to Self

Dear Self,

The gap between where you are and where God is taking you is called the stretch. The development and progress you want are in the stretch. The steps to fulfilling your calling and manifesting your destiny are in the stretch. The healthy relationships you desire are in the stretch. The impact you want to have in your community is in the stretch.

You will go through different seasons in life when you're stretched and feel uncomfortable but don't worry; God wants to use those seasons to develop you for your destiny. He wants to help you thrive! Therefore, today, I challenge you:

To say "YES" to God stretching you.

God is calling you to stretch past your fears, past your insecurities, and past your limits. He wants you to stretch to move forward with power and authority, which will bring you great joy and peace. Therefore, do not be surprised when you find yourself being stretched in challenging situations, where it feels as though the odds are against you and you don't see a way out.

When your circumstances seem dreadful, instead of being disheartened and thinking, "God, why me?" Get ready! You are in an ideal position for the Lord to show out in your life and elevate you to the next level. He is setting you up to show His favor in amazing ways. Your greatness is in the stretch!

With Love,

Self

22 | God's Higher Way

For as the heavens are higher than the earth, so are my ways higher than your ways and my thoughts than your thoughts. **Isaiah 55:9**

Answering God's call doesn't always make sense, and it's rarely convenient. But He has an excellent plan for our lives, and it's important to recognize His ways are higher than our ways.

Note to Self

Dear Self,

Have you ever been on one path of life, and just when you feel like things are going perfectly — BANG! — the Lord interrupts, asking you to stop and start something new?

My advice to you is to trust the Lord with all your heart and mind! Make room for Him to move in and through you, even if it feels like an interruption. Understand, His ways aren't like your ways. His thoughts are higher, which is why He doesn't ask you to understand Him but to trust Him. And as you choose to trust Him, He's going to astonish you!

With Love,

Self

SELF-REFLECTIONS

Think of the moment when you chose to follow Jesus. What did you understand about what it meant to be a believer?

___
___
___
___
___
___
___
___
___
___
___
___
___
___
___
___

What did you not realize?

23 | Celebrate!

Praise the Lord! Praise God in his sanctuary; praise him in his mighty heavens! Praise him for his mighty deeds; praise him according to his excellent greatness! Praise him with trumpet sound; praise him with lute and harp! Praise him with tambourine and dance; praise him with strings and pipe! Praise him with sounding cymbals; praise him with loud clashing cymbals! Let everything that has breath praise the Lord! Praise the Lord! **Psalm 150:1-6**

Our current society is losing its capacity for celebration. Instead of celebrating, we seek to be entertained or distracted. Celebration is an active state, an act of articulating admiration or thankfulness. To be entertained is a passive state. It is to receive personal preference afforded by an amusing act or a spectacle. Celebration is an encounter, giving kindness to the transcendent meaning of one's actions.

Note to Self

Dear Self,

Celebrate every small achievement and gain strength from the magnificence of celebrating. Understand, life is a celebration and each day offers a reason to rejoice.

- Celebrate the loveliness that surrounds you.

- Celebrate the wonder of life.
- Celebrate the beauty and miracle that you are.
- Celebrate the love God has for you.
- Celebrate others passionately.
- Celebrate the fact that your past mistakes are forgiven.
- Celebrate because you will win!
- Celebrate the little things as you go about your day.

Always remember regular, consistent celebration pulls us back to remembering God's goodness. Therefore, do not take today for granted. Make every moment count! And never forget:

You are not a problem to be tolerated. You are an asset to be desired, preserved, and celebrated.

With Love,

Self

Part 2: Soul Care…
MINDFUL OF YOUR WORLD

A DOUBTFUL MIND IS LIKE AN UNSETTLED WAVE IN THE SEA, TOSSED BY THE WIND.

24 | God Approves You

Let the one who boasts, boast in the Lord. For it is not the one who commends himself who is approved, but the one whom the Lord commends. **2 Corinthians 10:17-18**

We need to understand who we are and what we do are extraordinary and unique. Whether it's our gorgeous smiles, loving hugs, compassionate souls, incredible intellects, or our undeniable presence, everything we share has a ripple effect on every person around us. We matter in more ways than we could ever possibly imagine.

We have to believe that God has called us to go into the world in His name and not listen to the crippling labels and limitations forced on us by others. The world needs us to think big, show up boldly, share our gifts, and pursue our callings. The world needs what God has deposited in us.

God created us, approved of us, breathed life into us, and has plans to use us. We are a gift, an expression of who He is, and the calling on our lives will give birth to hope. The Lord has inspired us to move forward with power and authority for His glory.

Note to Self

Dear Self,

This concept is one of the most important things you could learn in your life: **You must learn to live without the approval of people.** Here is the reality, if your goal is to get the approval of people and God simultaneously, you won't.

Please understand that life is an ongoing process. Every day is an opportunity to learn something new. A chance to become who God created you to be. Therefore, when you feel unworthy, unloved, and unknown, you know the Creator of the world sees you and loves you, even with your flaws!

Your king, Jesus the Christ, shed His blood for you so that you could have your shame taken away. Never forget that God approves of you and loves you as His child. Now, go out and forge new paths and unleash new ideas. Don't limit your future by your ability because you serve a limitless God.

With Love,

Self

25 | Kingdom-driven Life

For the kingdom of God is not a matter of eating and drinking but of righteousness and peace and joy in the Holy Spirit. **Romans 14:17**

A kingdom-driven life means we have an unshakeable faith. The type of faith that is impossible to change, shake, or beat down. The kind of faith that is confident in knowing Jesus is our rock and mighty fortress.

A kingdom-driven life means discovering God's purpose and then finding our place in it. It means understanding that everything we have, all that we do, and every relationship we are involved in serves the greater purpose of advancing the Kingdom of God and the Lord's righteousness.

A kingdom-driven life will cause us to evaluate our lives, show us the proper adjustments to make, and it will cause us to grow in the knowledge of the Kingdom of God. It's time to start worshipping, working, and living like a kingdom-driven people. Because in the Kingdom of God, grace flourishes all the more so that grace might reign through righteousness, leading to eternal life through Jesus Christ our Lord.

Note to Self

Dear Self,

Did you know God chose you to do amazing things for His Kingdom? You are a vital part of a team assembled by the Lord to achieve His purposes. In fact, here are four specific purposes for why God chose you:

- **You were chosen to give God praise.**

  "The people whom I formed for myself that they might declare my praise." **Isaiah 43:21**

- **You were chosen to build a community.**

  "Therefore encourage one another and build one another up, just as you are doing." **1 Thessalonians 5:11**

- **You were chosen to be an example of Kingdom living.**

  "But our citizenship is in heaven…" **Philippians 3:20**

- **You were chosen to serve God and others.**

  "As each has received a gift, use it to serve one another, as good stewards of God's varied grace." **1 Peter 4:10**

God chose you, and with Him, you can do all things through Christ who strengthens you.

With Love,

Self

26 | Jesus, the Best Decision

Therefore, choose life, that you and your offspring may live, loving the Lord your God, obeying his voice and holding fast to him, for he is your life and length of days, that you may dwell in the land. **Deuteronomy 30:19-20**

Did you know good and bad decisions are usually based on how you feel, but godly choices are based on godly revelations, biblical truths, and your faith?

The good news is that you can start making better decisions by choosing Jesus.

- With Jesus as your focus, you can let go of the pain from a loss, you can let go of the frustration of not accomplishing your goals, and you can let go of the sorrow and negativity.
- With Jesus, you can embrace all you are and all you can be.
- With Jesus, nothing is hopeless.
- With Jesus, it is never too late.

You cannot change your yesterday, but with Jesus, the decisions you make right now can change your today.

Note to Self

Dear Self,

I want to encourage you to make a decision today, a decision that has the power to propel you into everything God wants you to do in your life. Today, decide to take complete control of your mind and govern your feelings according to the sovereignty of Christ. Yes, it will be challenging, but when you feel weak, He is strong. When you feel insignificant, He is mighty. The voice of doubt may seem loud, but you can overcome it. You can take its power away by choosing the voice of the Lord.

Trust in Jesus! Then move forward in faith and allow your faith to be filled with all kinds of possibilities because all things are possible through Christ. Jesus defeated the grave, so you do not have to stay in a place of defeat or discouragement. You can move forward with power and victory!

With Love,

Self

27 | Foundation of Wisdom

The fear of the LORD is the beginning of wisdom, and the knowledge of the Holy One is insight. **Proverbs 9:10**

Wisdom seems to be on the decline these days. Our society has a habit of putting a value on things that are trendy and instantaneous. Thus, we tend to neglect wisdom, which is traditional, modest, and slow. Furthermore, we are entranced by the audacity of youth rather than the prudence of maturity.

Proverbs 9:10 reminds us that wisdom is not something we gain on our own. Instead, true wisdom comes from knowing, adoring, reverencing, submitting to, and obeying God.

Over the years, I have learned that we will have a certain amount of joy and peace if we never seek guidance and wisdom from the world nor embrace the world's disobedient and self-centered ways. But, everlasting peace and joy are found when we meditate on the words of the Most-High God, day and night, and follow His instructions. In other words, the foundational point for obtaining wisdom is to be consumed with admiration for the Holy One.

Note to Self

Dear Self,

If you look at all the "facts" of life around you, achieving your goals and fulfilling your destiny can seem far out of reach. But if you focus on God and listen for His wisdom, nothing will be impossible for you! Therefore, live your complete life in reverent respect of God, seeking His guidance and glory in all you do. You must empty yourself of all your pride and allow the Holy Spirit to fill you with His wisdom. And if you lack wisdom, by faith, ask the Lord, who gives generously to all without reproach.

Please understand, those who have God's wisdom will show it in how they live. They will show it by the way they love and by the godly deeds done in humility. So, trust God to provide, and you will experience the peace of His wisdom, love, and gentleness. And always remember, as you worship God and study His commandments, you will receive revelation, understanding, and great wisdom.

With Love,

Self

28 | Have Confidence in God

In the fear of the Lord one has strong confidence, and his children will have a refuge. **Proverbs 14:26**

At the beginning of every breakthrough in our lives, fear will try to keep us from moving forward. But take heart and understand that courage is not the absence of fear but the ability to move forward despite it. We were created to walk in faith and confidence.

Even though there are storms in life, we must be confident that God has His hand upon us. We must walk in confidence, knowing God is with us, loves us, and wants the very best for us. It is much better to live out of a place of wholeness, confidence, and faith rather than to live out of insecurity and fear. Remember, fear focuses on our ability's inadequacy, but confidence focuses on the adequacy of God's sovereignty and lordship.

Therefore, we need to step forward in faith with absolute confidence in the new things God has in store for us. We are designed to win! We are created to be blessed!

Note to Self

Dear Self,

I know it can seem intimidating to exchange what you know for the great unknown. But you cannot continue to do things the same way and expect a different result. As hard as it is, you must make a decision that you are going to deal with your past, let God heal your wounds, confront your fears, and jump into the great unknown. Great faith is full of mystery and adventure.

Furthermore, if you build a relationship with God, He will fill you with hope and confidence. You will begin to realize that the Lord is more significant and more powerful than any situation you will ever encounter. Anything that comes your way and tempts you or causes any tragedy around you, you are capable of overcoming because the Lord's grace is sufficient for you. His power is made perfect in weakness.

God has so much more for you, and He has given you the Holy Spirit to empower you! So, don't throw away your confidence today because, in all things, you can achieve spiritual victory through Christ.

With Love,

Self

29 | When-Then Mindset

I will instruct you and teach you in the way you should go; I will counsel you with my eye upon you. **Psalm 32:8**

Here is the truth:

Success comes to those who take action.

Now, that doesn't mean we go off and try to force things to happen on our own; we must work with God. But too many dreams are lost because people sit around waiting for the perfect time and the best conditions. Our minds become flooded with reasons why something won't work, why we can't do it, why it's not realistic, why now isn't the best time, why another time will be perfect.

We call this the "When-Then" mentality, and it typically goes something like this: "When my children are grown, then I can travel. When I have more time, then I'll write a book. When work slows down… When I lose weight…

God has given us a choice to be the best version of ourselves. He has allowed us to be great, and becoming great is achieved by making God number one in our lives. Therefore, we must choose to have confidence in the Lord, keep His words near our hearts, and break free from the "when-then" trap and begin cultivating a vibrant, successful life of purpose and significance.

Note to Self

Dear Self

Every day, from this day forward, you must choose to do something about the dreams God has given you. Your greatness is never by chance; it results from God's love, great intention, genuine determination, and intelligent execution. Never allow other people's refusal to believe stop you from pursuing your dreams and God's calling on your life. Do not get caught in the "When-Then" trap.

When your goals and dreams are greater than those little excuses, your dreams and goals will become a reality, and success will follow. Here is a quote to remember: **Dreams becoming a reality is not a matter of chance but rather a matter of choice.**

With Love,

Self

30 | The Unexpected

Come now, you who say, "Today or tomorrow we will go into such and such a town and spend a year there and trade and make a profit"— yet you do not know what tomorrow will bring. What is your life? For you are a mist that appears for a little time and then vanishes. Instead you ought to say, "If the Lord wills, we will live and do this or that. **James 4:13-15**

There's not an individual on earth who hasn't found themselves at a point where life just didn't seem to make sense. Unexpected events, disappointments, disillusionment, disloyalty, and disease can fill us with fear, frustration, and even doubt. Yes, the unexpected can be hard to accept and even harder to walk through. But we're never alone. Our Jesus is here.

Therefore, when we encounter an unexpected situation, it is essential for us not to panic. We should close our eyes, take a deep breath, and pray. God will provide the solution. In fact, it is essential for us to believe that the same God who brought us this far will take us further. He will fulfill every promise He's given us.

Note to Self

Dear Self,

Tradition and routines are not life. Traditions and routines preserve life, but they do not give life. Life is here in this moment now. If truth be told, God never expected you to live a dull and predictable life, even though you work hard to create regular routines and traditions.

God has called you to live a life full of joy and sorrow, battles and celebrations, achievements and failures, ups and downs. He wants you to learn how to live expectantly during the unexpected to gain wisdom and understanding from every situation and challenge.

Life, a blessed life, is about who you are now, where the core of your soul lies at this very moment during the unexpected. Always remember this quote: **Living by faith means learning to expect God to do unexpected things and bring unexpected blessings into your life.** In other words, leave fear behind, move forward in faith, and embrace the adventure of the unexpected!

With Love,

Self

31 | Let God Be Big

Great is the Lord, and greatly to be praised, and his greatness is unsearchable. **Psalm 145:3**

When life feels too hard, when we are in the heat of the battle and stress mounts, sometimes we listen to the wrong voice and find ourselves forgetting how big our God is. Stop for a moment, and let's consider just how enormous God is because He's massive! And yet, the God of the universe, our Creator, the One who gave us breath, can be made big or small in the hearts of His people. Therefore, we can rest in knowing God is bigger and more powerful than us.

But just in case we still have trouble believing, here are two scriptures to back it up:

- *"He determines the number of the stars; he gives to all of them their names. Great is our Lord, and abundant in power; his understanding is beyond measure."* **Psalm 147:4-5**
- *"When I look at your heavens, the work of your fingers, the moon and the stars, which you have set in place, what is man that you are mindful of him, and the son of man that you care for him?"* **Psalm 8:3-4**

Note to Self

Dear Self,

Every time you thought there was no answer, the Lord answered you or gave you new, more intelligent questions to ask. Every time you thought you were out of options, the Lord opened an unseen path for you. Every time you thought you would fall apart, He held you together. Every time you thought you weren't enough, the Lord showed you that with Him, you were.

Consider that every time you go to sleep, God still is in control and in charge. When you're weary, He is strong. When political turmoil threatens your community, God stays upon His throne just like He did through other tumultuous times. The Lord is bigger than your fears, mistakes, and your disease.

So, today, take a step forward in faith and pursue your dreams. It may be challenging, but the Lord can move the mountains you cannot climb. Let God be big!

With Love,

Self

32 | Prayer: The Path of Life

Heavenly Father,

Keep me safe, Lord, for in You I have found shelter. You are my God and my counselor. I am no good separated from You, for Your mercy is my portion, and Your love is my prize. You have ordered my steps, so my joy will fall in pleasant places.

I will praise You, Oh God, forever and ever. I have set Your ways before me. You are my solid foundation, and I will not be shaken. My heart is glad, and my mind rejoices in Your goodness.

My mind is secure, for You will not abandon me nor let the enemy destroy me. You make known to me the path of life. An abundance of happiness is in Your presence. Eternal pleasures are in Your right hand.

Father, thank You for choosing me. You picked me out for Yourself as Your own, before the foundation of the world. You have destined and appointed me to come progressively to know Your will. Your Holy Spirit abides permanently in me and guides me into the complete truth.

I have the mind of Christ, and I will not be conformed to this world but be transformed by the renewing of my mind, so that I may discern what is the Your will — what is good and acceptable and perfect. So, Father, I have entered into that blessed rest by adhering, trusting, relying on You.

In Jesus' name, Amen.

SELF-REFLECTIONS

Why does God want you to depend on him and not yourself? In your current circumstances, what would surrendering to God look like?

_____

_____

_____

_____

_____

_____

_____

_____

_____

_____

33 | A Reminder to Trust

And those who know your name put their trust in you, for you, O Lord, have not forsaken those who seek you. **Psalm 9:10**

The key to overcoming worry, anxiety, or stress isn't doing everything perfectly or making sure everything around us is perfect. The reality is, there will always be things in our lives outside our control. Therefore, the key is to trust God's process, God's timing, God's provision, and know that God is in control.

The power of trusting God is something we should always take care to remember. Nonetheless, the act of trusting is so often easier said than done. Despair, disloyalty, or just the hopelessness that comes with this world will leave us feeling like the only individual we can trust is ourselves. However, when we cannot see a way out, we have to trust the character of God.

We have to trust that the God who gave us life is the same God who will help us thrive in life. Even when all we see is confusion, God is creating beautiful order. When all we see is the impossible, God is creating a miracle. The Lord's power will make a way even when the odds are stacked against us.

Note to Self

Dear Self,

Do you trust that where God is taking you is better than where you are? _____

Do you trust He is working all things for your good?
_____

When you trust God to do what He said He would do, you will not only experience peace; you are going to live in the fulfillment of His promises. But trust is like a muscle; the more you exercise it, the more it grows. Here are three exercises to trusting God more in your life:

1. Surrender all of your troubles to God.
2. Replace negative thoughts with positive ones.
3. Ask God to help you develop patience.

I want you always to remember that God is for you! You can surrender your life to Him, and He will make something spectacular out of it. He will comfort you and provide for you. Trust God's process, God's timing, and God's provision.

With Love,

Self

34 | Watch Your Mouth

Let no corrupting talk come out of your mouths, but only such as is good for building up, as fits the occasion, that it may give grace to those who hear. **Ephesians 4:29**

What are you declaring in your life? There is power and authority in the words we speak, and when we choose, by faith, to proclaim God's truth found in His Word, we have a chance to be part of transforming our world, our relationships, and ourselves.

Our voice is a powerful tool that God has given us, and we can either use it for our good and His glory, or we can abuse it and hurt ourselves and our loved ones with it. That is why we must declare God's Word over ourselves and the situations in our lives.

Note to Self

Dear Self,

The words you speak have so much power, affecting you and the people around you, revealing what is happening inside you. If you lose control of your tongue and do not select your words wisely, your life will be impacted and taken off course. In fact, the words you speak when you are faced with a situation that seems impossible have an enormous impact on the outcome of your situation. In other words, your future is set in motion by your words, so you must affirm positive words to enrich your life positively.

That's why I want to encourage you today to be aware of the words coming out of your mouth and speak life purposefully. The Bible shows you repeatedly how the tongue is a powerful tool that can both build up and tear down. Therefore, when you find yourself in the middle of an impossible situation, overwhelmed with the unknown and frustration surrounding you, you have an opportunity to speak life instead of death.

With the words you speak, you can activate the blessings of God in your life by declaring the truth of His Word over yourself and your circumstances. So, use your words to build relationships and not tear people down. You must talk less, listen more, and stop making excuses. Always remember, you frame your world with the words that you speak.

With Love,

Self

35 | Watch Your Focus

Set your minds on things that are above, not on things that are on earth.
Colossians 3:2

Sometimes we can get so caught up in what other people have done to us and how they've hurt us that it causes us to lose focus, and fear steals our joy. In fact, the more we reflect on something, the larger we perceive it to be. That is why we must have the proper perspective on our problems. We need to understand that no one is immune to fear. But the difference between living by fear and living by faith lies in our focus.

If we focus on things that did not happen for us or how someone was hateful towards us, those issues can seem so significant that they consume us. We get stuck in a painful place of unforgiveness. However, if we focus on Jesus and magnify Him, things will look simple, and we will be overwhelmed by His love and grace.

There is so much power gained or lost, depending on what we are focusing on. We must not focus on what is seen but focus on what is unseen. For what is seen is temporary, but what is unseen is eternal.

Note to Self

Dear Self,

The key isn't to look at your problems; it's to look higher to your Protector and Provider. When you make your problems your focus, that's when you'll find yourself gripped by fear. But when you make God bigger — and He is bigger — you'll find faith rising in your spirit, and you'll be ready to move forward into all He has for you! Therefore:

- Focus on the great things in your life.
- Focus on all the amazing things God has done for you.
- Think about what Jesus endured for you.
- Think about the Lord's faithfulness, His forgiveness toward you, and His deep, abiding love for you.
- Meditate on the goals, promises, and dreams God has given you, and magnify His holy name!

If things around you do not change, change your focus and change the things you are around!

With Love,

Self

36 | Leave the Past Behind

Remember not the former things, nor consider the things of old. Behold, I am doing a new thing; now it springs forth, do you not perceive it? I will make a way in the wilderness and rivers in the desert. **Isaiah 43:18-19**

Some of us take our past with us everywhere we go, dragging it along behind us.

Why do we do it?

Is it because it's familiar to us?

When individuals talk about their past, it seems to take on the characteristics of a real-life being. However, the past cannot breathe, talk, think, or act. Nonetheless, it is massively influential and can take over our future if we let it. Focusing on the past will undoubtedly limit our choices for the future.

Note to Self

Dear Self,

Do not get trapped by your past. Decide you will no longer allow the doubt and frustration of your past to define your future. Proverbs says, **"Let your eyes look straight ahead; fix your gaze directly before you" (Proverbs**

4:25). It would be best if you fixed your eyes on the things directly before you. You must have the mindset and willpower to say that the things of your past will no longer capture your focus. And though you don't want to hurt anyone's feelings, you might have to separate yourself from some friends and some things to pursue the Kingdom of God wholeheartedly.

I want to encourage you to fix your eyes on King Jesus and commit to doing whatever it takes to draw closer to Him, removing anything that has held you back. Choose to fill your heart with faith because you serve a mighty and strong God, and He can do more than you could ever ask or hope.

So, starting today, leave your past behind by letting go of the old and who you used to be. Embrace the new and who God wants you to be. And always remember, open your mind and your heart so you will be free to hold the blessings and promises of God.

With Love,

Self

37 | We Serve A Limitless God

What is impossible with man is possible with God. **Luke 18:27**

The God we serve is limitless! He created the world, keeps it all together, and has made and allows each of us to play a unique part in His redemption story. This strong, powerful, and mighty God is not distant or detached but ever-present, loving, and compassionate.

We can walk and not be faint. We can run and not be weary. Here's why:

We have the Spirit of God with us! And life with Him is a life of endless wonder and limitless possibility.

The Lord, our God, can solve any problem, heal any broken heart, reconcile any relationship, and forgive any sin. Our loving God can stretch any budget, feed the hungry, put clothes on our bodies, and free any captive. Our heavenly Father can break any habit, cure any disease, and give sight to the blind. Here is the truth: **There is simply nothing our God cannot do!**

In other words, if we believe God has the power to create and sustain the universe, then surely there is nothing in our lives that is beyond His authority to mend, heal or restore.

Note to Self

Dear Self,

God loves you! God has forgiven you! God will provide for you, so you do not need to have fear. God will take care of yesterday's failures, today's frustrations, and tomorrow's uncertainties.

The Lord has unlimited resources, unlimited energy, unlimited knowledge, and unlimited time. Therefore, starting today, stop seeing the difficulty in light of your resources because you serve a limitless God!

You are a child of God, which means you are royalty and have access to unlimited resources so that you can do His good works and impact the world. It is time for you to live courageously and boldly. Let this verse encourage you today:

If the Spirit of him who raised Jesus from the dead dwells in you, he who raised Christ Jesus from the dead will also give life to your mortal bodies through his Spirit who dwells in you (Romans 8:11).

With Love,

Self

38 | Child of the Most-High God

So God created man in his own image, in the image of God he created him; male and female he created them. **Genesis 1:27**

Do you ever feel like everyone is shaming everyone these days? Between social media, school, work, the press, it's hard to step outside of it all. Nonetheless, even in the middle of all this blame, criticism, and condemnation, we know that we are all children of God. We are children of a God who loves and treasures us. We are chosen, sought after, and adored.

Let's think about that for a second! What marvelous love the heavenly Father has given us, that we should be called God's children! If truth be told, the world does not know us and is angry with us because the world does not know Him.

When we live as Jesus called us to — letting our love lift others up — we are going to experience the Father's best! Understand, we were created to bear the image of God. What an honor, privilege, and example of just how highly we are valued and esteemed!

Note to Self

Dear Self,

It is time for you to declare that you are one of God's most fabulous creations. He had visions about you long before you were born. God is pouring Himself into you, shaping every part of your life into a fantastic work of art. Therefore, be courageous, and accept these never-failing truths:

- You are anointed by God.
- You are victorious through Jesus Christ.
- You are a member of a chosen race, a royal priesthood, a holy nation.
- You have been given a spirit of power, love, and self-control.
- You are a one-of-a-kind expression of God's glory.
- You are fearfully and wonderfully made to impact the world!

No matter what you go through, because you are a child of the Most-High God, the Lord will give you strength that you cannot explain, the courage you did not know you had, and favor you did not see coming. Let no one dim your light!

With Love,

Self

39 | Original Masterpiece

For you formed my inward parts; you knitted me together in my mother's womb. I praise you, for I am fearfully and wonderfully made. Wonderful are your works; my soul knows it very well. **Psalm 139:13-14**

None of our past situations and mistakes have ever changed God's perception of our precious worth. No matter how mortified or ashamed we may feel by what we have experienced in this world, God has always had a plan to restore us to our original and priceless value. His eye has been focused on us since the day we were conceived in our mother's womb, and His desire has always been to bring us back to the image in which He created us! Only when we understand our actual value can we begin to have and do all God has for us.

When anything is made to be an original, it automatically has a significant value attached to it! Understand, nothing else in creation was created in God's image, which means we were made on purpose, for a purpose. And no matter what our past might say, we are God's masterpiece — priceless and treasured in every way!

Note to Self

Dear Self,

You have become the Lord's poetry, a beautiful work of art that will fulfill the destiny He has given you, for you are joined with Jesus, the Anointed One. Even before you were born, God planned, in advance, your purpose and the good works you would do to fulfill it! Therefore, refuse to devalue your worth by living as a poor copy of someone else or living for someone else! Let the uniqueness of your individuality shine bright so Jesus will be magnified! Recognize your unique personality and characteristics are qualities people need. You can inspire others to greatness and motivate them to be all they were created to be for God's glory.

If you are going to be all God created you to be, you have to start by being okay with who you are today. You will get better, stronger, and wiser because God's fingerprints are all over you. The Lord has called you to be different, to stand against the grain. He has called you to be a city on a hilltop and hope when the world lacks hope. Stop trying to fit in because you were created to stand out!

With Love,

Self

40 | Certain Truths

Jesus Christ is the same yesterday and today and forever. **Hebrews 13:8**

There is a lot of uncertainty in our world, and at some point, everything in this world will fail. However, there is one certain truth that can transform the way we live and that truth is, as Believers-in-Christ, we are citizens of Heaven. And with this citizenship, we each have certain rights and privileges. Philippians 3:20 says, **"But our citizenship is in heaven, and from it we await a Savior, the Lord Jesus Christ."**

Here are a few rights and privileges we have in Christ:

- The enemy is under our feet (Romans 16:20).
- We can do all things through Him who strengthens us (Philippians 4:13).
- We are more than conquerors through Him who loved us (Romans 8:37).
- We have access to every spiritual blessing in Him (Ephesians 1:3).

"And you will know the truth, and the truth will set you free" (John 8:32)

Note to Self

Dear Self,

Let these truths encourage you:

- There is no bondage Jesus cannot break.
- There is no need Jesus cannot meet.
- There is no enemy Jesus cannot defeat.
- There is no mountain Jesus cannot move.
- There is no relationship Jesus cannot restore.
- There is no person Jesus cannot save.
- There is no chaos from which Jesus cannot bring peace.
- There is no sin that Jesus cannot forgive.
- There is no promise too hard for Jesus to fulfill.
- There is no prayer too small for Jesus to answer.
- There is no disease Jesus cannot heal.
- There is no heart Jesus cannot mend.

With Love,
Self

41 | Be Blessed Abundantly

And God is able to bless you abundantly, so that in all things at all times, having all that you need, you will abound in every good work. **2 Corinthians 9:8**

Jesus came, died, and conquered the grave to give us an abundant life, and He wants us to live it!

Something to Contemplate:

- How has God blessed you in the past?
- How is God blessing you in this season of your life?
- How do you expect God to bless you in the future?

Note to Self

Dear Self,

In all things, at all times, for all you need, God is able and desires to bless you beyond what you can imagine. So, regardless of what you have experienced in your past or the challenges surrounding you today, believe in the Lord and take Him at His Word because He is faithful to His promises. God loves you with endless love, and you were put on this planet for a life of abundance, adventure, and purpose. You will be blessed abundantly!

With Love,

Self

Something to Attempt:

Write down ways in which God is blessing you now. If it is appropriate, share with someone close to you. Then, thank the Lord for His goodness and His faithfulness to you.

42 | When Facing Opposition

"Blessed are those who are persecuted for righteousness' sake, for theirs is the kingdom of heaven. "Blessed are you when others revile you and persecute you and utter all kinds of evil against you falsely on my account. Rejoice and be glad, for your reward is great in heaven, for so they persecuted the prophets who were before you. **Matthew 5:10-12**

Here are a few things we must learn while we are following the Lord:

- Closed doors do not mean that God is not opening other doors.
- The existence of a battle does not mean the absence of God in the war.
- Trials do not mean we are out of the will of God. They often mean we are precisely in the center of God's will.
- The opposition does not prevent the presence of God in our lives. It creates an opportunity to prove the presence of God.

When we decide to live our lives pursuing our divine assignments, pursuing our God-given purposes with everything we've got, we will face opposition from others.

We will receive resistance, and one of their weapons of choice is condemnation. In fact, when we pursue God's will for our lives, we may even face rejection from the people we love dearly. But like Jesus, who faced opposition and rejection everywhere He went, no weapon formed against us will prosper. Not even the worst of insults or criticism.

Note to Self

Dear Self,

Did you know that seeing the problem is rarely the problem? Rather than seeing a problem as a burdensome force of opposition, take the time to see problems as opportunities to learn, grow, or adjust in a way that leaves you better off than before the issue existed.

If you align your heart with the will of God, you cannot and will not be stopped! The opposition you experience will become a sign that you are doing something courageous and impactful. And always remember, there will always be a lot of pain and brokenness in the world, but know Christ is right there with you. And in Him, you have the victory!

With Love,

Self

43 | Prayer: Save Me

Heavenly Father,

I will praise You with my whole heart. I will tell the world about all Your wonders. I will be glad and rejoice in Your love. I will worship Your name!

As for me, Lord, please save me!

You know all my troubles and sufferings. You have been there all along, even though I sometimes don't feel you. Deep waters surround my heart and soul, and I cannot find a foothold. I feel like I am sinking as life's floods overwhelm me.

Oh God, I feel like I'm drifting away from the person who you want me to be. I am exhausted and weary from crying out for help. Lord, I cannot see You, for all the tears have blurred my vision; I no longer see your compassion or grace.

Father, You already know the pain in my heart, but I give it to You. You see the suffering in my mind, but I give You my soul. You know my enemies try to destroy me with lies, but I give them to You. Even the people I love occasionally misunderstand me. No matter what is said to me or about me, I give their accusations to You.

Lord, draw near to my soul and redeem it. Hear me with Your kindness and gentleness. With Your never-ending, unconditional love, pull me from the deep and rescue me. Do not let the waves overwhelm me.

Answer my prayer, Oh Lord. For Your love never fails, and Your great mercy will never give up on me. My hope is only in You. You are my God, and I am your child through my faith in Jesus Christ, Your Anointed One.

It is in Jesus' name, I say, Amen.

44 | Is God Waiting On You?

For by grace you have been saved through faith. And this is not your own doing; it is the gift of God, not a result of works, so that no one may boast. For we are his workmanship, created in Christ Jesus for good works, which God prepared beforehand, that we should walk in them.
Ephesians 2:8-10

Are we waiting on God, or is God waiting on us?

None of us likes waiting. We want what we want, and we want it now. Yet as Christians, we are constantly reminded to wait on God. It's easy to say but can be very difficult actually to do.

Waiting on God and His will to take place in our lives is essential. It is vital as believers to wait and not get ahead of the Lord. But if we are honest, waiting on God can be painful, and the longer it takes, the worse the mental agony gets — we pray, we cry, we wait. Then we cry, pray and wait some more. However, waiting passively for God to do something supernatural is not typically how God works.

Sometimes God is waiting on us to take a step forward with faith, and by faith – and then and only then –

do we begin to see the work of God's hand in our lives. For God to order our steps, we have to start stepping.

Note to Self

Dear Self,

Are you the answer to your prayers? When you are praying and asking God to do something, do you think He is waiting for you to partner with Him to do it?

Move forward in faith! Understand, the Lord is waiting for you. Start where you are, and God will meet you right there. Pursue those dreams in your less-than-perfect circumstances, and just watch what God does with them!

As imperfect as you are, the Lord will use you in your less-than-perfect circumstances to do His great work. You won't know what He has planned for you unless you give Him the chance to show you by trusting Him and stepping out in faith. Furthermore, you must prioritize seeking God for solutions in the world, so ask the Lord how you can be a part of the solution while you're seeking Him. If you acknowledge Him in all of your ways, He will straighten your crooked path, and you will walk in the fullness of Christ.

With Love,

Self

45 | Obedience: Is It Worth It?

If you are willing and obedient, you shall eat the good of the land.
Isaiah 1:19

Let's take a look at a verse in the book of Joshua. Joshua 6:2 says, **"Then the LORD said to Joshua, See, I have delivered Jericho into your hands, along with its king and its fighting men."** Did you notice the past tense of that verse? Jericho had not even been defeated, yet the Lord had already given Joshua and the nation of Israel the victory.

If we move past the passage's surface level, we can see the real battle was not with the people of Jericho. It was in the hearts of the people of Israel. Would they believe and trust God? Would they obey the command of the Lord and walk around the walls of Jericho even though it did not make sense?

We are all called to obedience, not convenience. We are called to accomplish the assignments and plans the Lord has mapped out for our lives. Our calling originates with the Father, and He finds us wherever we are to invite us to step into all that He has for us. Our responsibility is to obey and get to work right where He has us today.

Note to Self

Dear Self,

Do you know how God measures your love? It's not by what you say. God measures your love by your obedience. Proverbs 3:6 says, ***"In all your ways acknowledge him, and he will make straight your paths."*** In other words, God will open doors, put the right people in your path and orchestrate the entire thing on your behalf. All you have to do is move when He tells you to move and stay when He tells you to stay!

Obedience may not always seem like a fun option, but it is still worth it. There will be times you will not understand God's instructions, and there will be times you will. But whether you understand or not, you need to obey.

Obedience is better than sacrifice, and it is the premise behind all of His promises. If you want to enjoy His promises so you can bear good fruit in your business, health, with your family, and friendships, you will have to follow His instructions. With a renewed mind and obedience, the Lord will shower you with blessings and favor beyond your wildest dreams.

With Love,

Self

46 | Prayer: Obedient Heart

Heavenly Father,

Thank You for Your love and truth. I also want to thank You for the desire to transform me into the image and likeness of Your Son, King Jesus. Lord, I depend on You for all things. I want to live a godly life and have a heart of humility and obedience to Your word.

I have realized that people come and go. Causes rise and fall. Emotions are temporary. But following You, by my faith in the resurrected Christ, is a lifestyle that requires wholehearted surrender and obedience.

I have learned through your holy scriptures that if I have a willing heart to obey You, I will feast on the blessings of an abundant harvest. But if I am stubborn and refuse to obey, my disobedience will bring destruction and death. Therefore, help me take every thought captive and surrender my heart and life to You in faithful obedience and godly humility.

I want to be drawn closer to You as You do good work in me and as I do good work in the lives of others. May Your indwelling Holy Spirit prompt me, guide me, encourage me, and teach me. May Your mighty Spirit wrap around me and anoint me as a messenger to preach the good news of the Kingdom of God to the poor and brokenhearted.

Father, I surrender all I am to You, and I surrender my plans and dreams to You so that You can give me Your plans for my life. I pray that I may walk in the newness of love and humble obedience all the days of my life. You are the Holy One worthy of my worship, praise, attention, and affection.

It is in Jesus' name I pray, Amen.

47 | Done Decently and In Order

But all things should be done decently and in order. ***1 Corinthians 14:40***

It seems the Apostle Paul had heard reports about the confusion and disorder in the Corinthian church. After detailing rules for an orderly community of Believers throughout 1 Corinthians 14, Paul summed things up with this warning to do everything "decently and in order."

It is human nature to resist imposed order. Although structure and order come naturally for some, it doesn't come without a fight for most individuals. However, when we work to have order in our lives, we create the ability to transcend the routine and produce spiritual fruit in our lives. Why? It is because the Lord is a God of order. Everything He does involves order and structure.

Note to Self

Dear Self,

Today, there are so many things globally, fighting for your attention and pulling you in a million different directions. Nonetheless, you must focus on the promises of God and His Kingdom and not the world's problems. When your focus is on God first and His divine order and structure, you will begin to imitate Jesus and become Christ-like. Therefore, you must wake up and give thanks to your Maker before starting your day because it creates order.

Any time you make space for order and structure in your life, you can see beyond the confusion and disorder of life and peer into the character of the Lord. In other words, you cannot just fit God in your schedule; you must build your schedule around Him and make Him the center of it all regardless of what is happening around you. Remember this statement: **Do the right things in the right order, and you'll be pleased with the right results.**

With Love,

Self

48 | Change Your Attitude

Do all things without grumbling or disputing, that you may be blameless and innocent, children of God without blemish in the midst of a crooked and twisted generation, among whom you shine as lights in the world, holding fast to the word of life, so that in the day of Christ I may be proud that I did not run in vain or labor in vain. **Philippians 2:14-15**

Let me save you a Google search and explain the difference between attitude and behavior. Attitude shows how individuals think, feel, and tend to behave towards people and things. Behavior is an activity or an action done. It occurs after the attitude. Let me say it this way: To put forth positive and inspiring action, we must have a positive and inspiring attitude because our attitude serves as the mental filter through which we see the world.

Therefore, today is a good day for us to have an attitude of gratitude, an attitude of hope, an attitude of love. We should have an attitude of faith, with expectancy, that we will receive every blessing God has in store for us. And we should never forget that our attitude toward life will determine life's attitude towards us.

Note to Self

Dear Self,

I know you have faced some difficulties, and there have been situations out of your control. You have had several obstacles that seem impossible to overcome. But focus on the promises of God and smile. Understand, your attitude toward life will frequently determine how you get through life. Jesus Christ has already overcome the world and promised you victory. It is time for you to have a winning attitude and walk in the boldness of Christ!

If you're not proactive, the wrong mindset will show up. Therefore, starting today, find the determination, perseverance, and tenacity to have a positive attitude. Maintain an attitude of gratitude and thanksgiving for who God is, all that He has done, and all He continues to do. Your attitude will regulate your altitude; it will control how high or how low you go. Your attitude will determine how far in life you will go. With a great attitude, you have an opportunity to look for a miracle during the battle.

With Love,

Self

Part 3: Soul Care...
DISCOVER YOUR GREATEST STRENGTH

PRAY AND KEEP MOVING FORWARD! THE RESISTANCE IS BUILDING YOUR RESILIENCE.

49 | The Lord is Our Helper

Fear not, for I am with you; be not dismayed, for I am your God; I will strengthen you, I will help you, I will uphold you with my righteous right hand. **Isaiah 41:10**

We have grown so accustomed to having apps and online systems to do the work for us that we think building our character occurs the same way. On the contrary, there are no apps for building godly character. The truth is, it's a process. And while sometimes it's challenging work, it's divine work — obeying the Lord, going the distance in our race, and telling others about the healing and freedom found by seeking the Kingdom of God.

Today, decide to be all God has created and called you to be, no matter how intimidating the path may be. He is the God of the impossible, and He is ready to release miracles on your behalf! Why? Because the Lord is our friend and our comforter. He is our joy and our hope, our defense and defender – our provider and supporter. God is our anchor and assurance. The Lord is our helper!

Note to Self

Dear Self,

The Lord is the creator and supporter of your soul. He will save you by His name, for His name's sake. Therefore, no matter where we are in life, don't give up. Please don't run from your problems. Don't try to escape. Ask God for help and trust Him to provide.

The Lord is your very present help in your time of need. Others may have left you, disappointed you, and not come through for you, but God will never leave or forsake you! That means He is with you at all times.

So, reach out to Him more often, lean on Him each day and allow Him to be your helper — because your help comes from Him! And when you do this, you will experience the peace of His wisdom and favor.

Lastly, give thanks to the Lord, for He is good, and His love endures forever. If God is for you, then who can be against you?

With Love,

Self

50 | Delightfully Made

The Spirit of God has made me, and the breath of the Almighty gives me life. **Job 33:4**

God says we were designed and made to do good works in Christ, works prepared before the creation of the world, which means God created us and for His purposes. So, no matter how we were born, no matter the particulars of our birth, we each were chosen in eternity long before we ever arrived at this point in time. Until we understand that, life will never make sense.

Let me keep this simple; we are not accidents! Our births were no mistakes or mishaps, and our lives are no fluke of nature. Please understand there are accidental parents, but there are no accidental births. There are illegitimate parents, but there are no illegitimate children. There are unplanned pregnancies, but there are no unpurposed people.

God prescribed every single detail of our bodies. He intentionally chose the color of our skin, the type of hair we would have, and every other feature. He also determined the uniqueness of our personalities so we can impact this generation.

Note to Self

Dear Self,

It is vital for you to know this: **God delights in all of His children, and He delights in you!**

- You are God's beautiful masterpiece!
- You are God's unique vessel!
- You are God's workmanship!

When God made you, He took into account your failures and even your sins. God never does anything accidentally, and He never makes mistakes. He has a reason for everything He creates.

Your gifts, abilities, and talents were given to you for a purpose, to help advance the Kingdom of God here on earth. You have been designed uniquely to serve a purpose that you can fulfill only by being your unique self. God has placed a mark of excellence upon you! You are not ordinary; you are extraordinary. You are not lucky; you are loved!

With Love,

Self

51 | Rest in the Work of Jesus

Come to me, all who labor and are heavy laden, and I will give you rest. Take my yoke upon you, and learn from me, for I am gentle and lowly in heart, and you will find rest for your souls. For my yoke is easy, and my burden is light. **Matthew 11:28-30**

The Apostle Paul was devoted, passionate, and energetic in fulfilling the Mosaic law. He lived a religious life. Paul had all of the proper credentials and followed all the guidelines and rules.

When Paul was awestruck and captivated by Jesus Christ, he found and learned he could access the authority and the resurrecting power of Jesus Christ to help him press forward. He no longer had to work for the victory; he could work from victory.

When we purposefully focus on the finished work of Jesus Christ, then we enter the realm of spiritual rest that God intended for us. When we do this, we can start and finish our days working from a place of joy, peace, and victory. For anyone who enters Christ's rest also rests from their works.

Note to Self

Dear Self,

It's no secret that you have a lot on your plate each day, and the Lord wants you to be able to do all that you desire. But you need supernatural rest to do it, and you can only get this by studying the scriptures and spending time in the presence of the Lord.

You need to get to that place where you can rest in Christ and get your identity and value in Him, not other people. You have to make what Jesus did for you more significant than what anybody has done to you. And you have to make what Jesus said about you more important than what anyone else said.

Therefore, when you feel weary, go to Jesus. When you feel burdened, go to Jesus. When you need rest, go to Jesus. He is waiting for you, just as you are. There is peace, comfort, and solace in Jesus Christ.

I need you always to remember: **The same Spirit that raised Christ from the dead lives inside you.** So, you can do all things through Him according to His will.

With Love,

Self

52 | Victory Is Our Heritage

No weapon that is fashioned against you shall succeed, and you shall refute every tongue that rises against you in judgment. This is the heritage of the servants of the Lord and their vindication from me, declares the Lord. **Isaiah 54:17**

Are you a servant of the Lord? If so, victory is your heritage!

Note to Self

Dear Self,

Most great accomplishments do not look encouraging in the beginning. Why? Because there cannot be glory without a struggle, nor achievement without a challenge. But you have a heritage of victory, a heritage that puts you on the pedestal of success.

When God gives you dreams and goals, understand it will take effort and time. It may be costly, inconvenient, or uncomfortable to complete, but stay strong. When you are at your lowest point, do not give up! When everything you have tried has failed, know you are close to winning; you are close to your breakthrough because the victory belongs to you.

The enemy has tried and will continue to try to delay your blessings while you struggle, grow frustrated, and get weary. Nevertheless, in the end, he cannot win! Therefore, there is no reason for you to live under a victim mentality because no matter what has consumed your past, Christ made you victorious when He laid down His life for you!

So, speak victory out of your mouth until you have the victory in your life. Stay encouraged and inspired! Rise up in royalty and take your place. You will be blessed far beyond your natural ability.

Walk in the victory standing before you and be the victor you are called to be. You have the power to choose wholeness and peace of mind. You can do all things through Christ who strengthens you. Nothing can stop you!

Thanks be to God, who gives you the victory through your Lord, Jesus Christ.

With Love,

Self

53 | Realizing You Matter

For you formed my inward parts; you knitted me together in my mother's womb. I praise you, for I am fearfully and wonderfully made. Wonderful are your works; my soul knows it very well. **Psalm 139:13-14**

We have tremendous influence in this world. Which means we are not invisible! We matter because God has chosen us to be His representative and carry His authority on the earth. We were created to do something remarkable in this world that will leave an influence of hope for others and comfort to those people we can help.

Note to Self

Dear Self,

You have been helping people for a long time now, but you feel overlooked and unappreciated for what you have done. God wants you to know that you matter and don't let anyone tell you any different. The hours you've put in, the kindness you've shown — you have made such a difference in the hearts of the people around you, and God is working through you in more ways than you realize.

You are the only you in the entire universe, and that makes you unique. No one else could ever be you, and that is your power. You have gifts to bring the world and changes to inspire. Once again, no matter what anyone says, you matter!

God's grace and favor are going to position you in places you never thought were possible. Therefore, you will need to be a good steward of your influence and keep a heart of compassion because your fingerprints will never fade from the lives you touch.

You are an individual of destiny, so look for ways to operate in your place of influence. Focus on creating an atmosphere of love, joy, and peace by using your words and gifts to inspire and empower others. God has poured out His love on you richly through Jesus Christ, your Savior. You have a right to be you, and it is a blessing for others to be around you.

With Love,

Self

54 | What You Do Matters

But as it is, God arranged the members in the body, each one of them, as he chose. If all were a single member, where would the body be? As it is, there are many parts, yet one body. **1 Corinthians 12:18-20**

We often walk by those who need help instead of helping like the good Samaritan. However, by serving others, our God is glorified, and He will bless our lives in return. Therefore, what we do matters!

- Our inspiration matters
- Our compassion matters
- Our generosity matters
- Our love matters
- Our service matters
- Our hospitality matters
- Our patience matters
- Our forgiveness matters

The Bible shows us that we are part of the body of Christ, and everything we do impacts and influences the entire body. Therefore, just because it isn't acknowledged does not mean it isn't on God's radar. What we do matters to God!

Note to Self

Dear Self,

In God's kingdom, you have a place, a purpose, a role, and an assignment to accomplish, and this gives your life great significance and extraordinary value, no matter how discouraged you may feel right now. You are not God's child by service, but as God's child, you were created for service. In other words, you serve God by serving others! Therefore, whether your actions are acknowledged by others or not, they're still on God's radar.

God has carefully designed you and placed you in the body of Christ to function as He desires. Your treasures, talents, and time are required for the body of Christ to advance the Kingdom of God. Anytime you use your God-given abilities to help others, you are fulfilling your divine assignment. So, embrace the place God has set you in today and ask Him to reveal a greater revelation of His purpose and plan for you. He loves you and has great things in store for you!

With Love,

Self

55 | It Does Not Matter

Now faith is the assurance of things hoped for, the conviction of things not seen. **Hebrews 11:1**

If God said it, God will do it!

It doesn't matter what storm we are in. It doesn't matter how dark the night is. It doesn't matter what size our giants are. What matters is the size of our God, and there is not a person on earth or demon in hell that can hold us back from God's plan, purpose, and promises.

Therefore, here are four tips to becoming a person of great faith while pursuing a great purpose with an extraordinary dream:

1. Remember how God has helped you in the past.
2. Use the tools that God has given you now.
3. Ignore the haters and doubters.
4. Expect God to help you for His glory.

By fixing our eyes on the Kingdom of God and not on our circumstances, we make God more prominent and allow Him to work on our behalf in extraordinary ways.

Note to Self

Dear Self

Haters are like crickets; they make a lot of noise you can hear, but you never see them. Then, when you walk right by them, they are quiet. Nonetheless, there are not enough haters in the world to hinder God's plan for your life! Therefore, stop worrying about the haters and stop asking permission to follow your dreams.

You will always have critics who think you are not enough, but you are not what the critics say you are; you are enough! In fact, it does not matter whether people believe in you or not. It is your job to live by faith and not by sight. God will handle the rest, and He will order your steps.

Love yourself and believe in yourself. You are one of a kind, and you are not alone. The Holy Spirit is with you every step of the way in life, no matter how gloomy, lonely, or disturbing those steps may be. Always remember, to achieve your destiny, you will have to step off the cliff and dive headfirst into a river of faith, knowing that if you have trouble swimming, Jesus is your life jacket.

With Love,

Self

56 | Prayer: God My Protector

Heavenly Father,

There are always going to be people in my life who misunderstand me and people who don't like me. There will always be people who criticize me, judge me, emotionally attack me, and spread rumors about me.

Therefore, I come to You today, bowing in my heart, asking for protection from the evil one and from people who are trying to hurt me. Surround me with Your divine hedge of protection because many individuals are rising against me! Many are saying in my presence, "You will not win; you are not great!"

You, my God, are an armor surrounding me and the lifter of my soul. Watch over my journey and guide me with your love through the hidden snares of life. Encompass me with Your strength and Your might. I cry out to You, my Lord, with my voice, and I know You will answer me from Your holy throne.

I lie down and sleep in peace, for You sustain me. Help me keep my focus on You, especially in times of rejection. Help me remember that You can use all things for my good and Your glory. Give me a heart that hopes and takes away the desire to lean on my own understanding.

Today I choose to walk and live under the safety of You, The Most-High. Thank You for Your protection, provision, and presence! Empower me to see the purpose You have for me through fresh eyes and help me to walk confidently in it. Let Your blessing be on Your people, Your children, who are called by Your name.

In Jesus' name, I pray, Amen.

57 | In Due Season

And let us not grow weary of doing good, for in due season we will reap, if we do not give up. **Galatians 6:9**

When we confuse due dates with due seasons, we may think God's timing is off, and we set ourselves up for disappointment. But the truth is God is never early, and He is never late. He is always on time in the correct season.

Every farmer knows that if we sow in one season, we will reap in another season. If we plant in the Fall, we will harvest in the Spring. Therefore, how we respond to someone or an issue right now will undoubtedly impact and influence the future. If we respond appropriately, with the love and grace of Christ, in our right now season, God's blessings will fall upon us soon.

Note to Self

Dear Self,

I know it's tough to keep at something when you don't see any results. But there is a purpose to the process that God calls you to and brings you through. Therefore, no matter which season you are in, there are three questions you must ask yourself to help you reap the blessing of God in your next season.

1. What can I learn in this season of my life?
2. What can I enjoy in this season of my life?
3. What can I do to help others in this season of my life?

You must evaluate everything you have going on in your life. You must evaluate what experiences you are holding on to. You must evaluate how you use your abilities, talents, gifts, and energy to help others. You must plant good seeds that promote growth, and that will help you manifest your destiny.

Let me encourage you today to remain persistent in the things you are doing, not for your own glory, but for the Lord's and the expansion of His Kingdom. Start trusting in God's perfect timing and shift your heart and mind to adjust to His timing methods. Keep expecting and believing that your due season is coming. For in due season, you will reap!

With Love,

Self

58 | God Must Come First

But seek first the kingdom of God and his righteousness, and all these things will be added to you. **Matthew 6:33**

Suppose we want to experience real security in our life. In that case, we have to form the habit of putting God first in everything in our lives — our conversations, how we spend our time, what we do with our finances — everything! We must keep our eyes focused on God and learn to love and be content with His plan and His calling for our lives.

Note to Self

Dear Self,

Take a minute to think about your current priorities; what are they?

Many of the conflicts you have, anxieties you experience, and overwhelming feelings you encounter are because you have compartmentalized your life. You fit the Lord into your priorities rather than putting Him first, at the center of everything you do. When you seek His Kingdom first, He then adds whatever you need. He doesn't forget your needs, deny them, or ignore them. He provides for each one.

To truly put God first, you have to let go of what others think. Abide in the Lord's Word. Listen to His voice. Pursue a deep relationship with Him. Because as you seek Him, you're going to find Him, and He's going to show you the incredible life He has for you!

By putting God first, I am confident that everything is going to work out for your good. Here is a quote to remember:

Self-focus limits people who only trust in themselves. People who focus and trust in God first and make Him their foundation are limitless! So, the key to the Lord's provision is to put Him first.

Lastly, I want to encourage you to begin expecting God in your everyday life. He wants to walk with you and show you new things every day. And that means today!

With Love,

Self

59 | Don't Settle for Less

Oh, taste and see that the Lord is good! Blessed is the man who takes refuge in him! **Psalm 34:8**

Too many of us settle for less than the Lord intended because we're waiting for somebody to give us permission to flourish; we're waiting for somebody to give us permission to be productive, to multiply our gifts and abilities, to increase our capacity for impact.

It is time for us to put our faith in God's power and take advantage of the opportunities He gives us. If we refuse to settle for a life of mediocrity, we will be able to pursue the excellence God has in store for us. We will be able to fulfill our greatest potential. We will live fearlessly in the face of difficulty.

Note to Self

Dear Self,

You can be who God created you to be and do what God has called you to do. I believe that with all my heart. But first, you have to seek His Kingdom, and then you have to get out of your comfort zone and take the risks God calls you to take. You have to be on the lookout for divine appointments because He is getting ready to promote you.

There are so many things that can influence your future, and all too often, these influences will try to distract you from your destiny. And that distraction will make it comfortable for you to settle for less than what God has for you. But God is faithful to keep all of His promises, and He has far more for you than what you are experiencing. If you agree, then join me by saying this prayer:

Heavenly Father,

I want to reflect Your glory in my life, in my relationships, in my work, and in my finances. Fill me with Your power to believe in more incredible things and never settle for less than what You want for me. Furthermore, I will stop waiting for permission to be great. I will confidently step into Your calling and commit to growing and going wherever You lead me to go. It is in the name of Jesus that I pray, Amen.

If you prayed that prayer in sincere faith, then rest in Jesus because it's in Him, you have the victory!

With Love,

Self

60 | Poised for a Resurrection

Blessed be the God and Father of our Lord Jesus Christ! According to his great mercy, he has caused us to be born again to a living hope through the resurrection of Jesus Christ from the dead. **1 Peter 1:3**

While we might be in a battle against the enemy today, we need to always remember that our God has already won the war. And through Jesus Christ, the Anointed One, we have been born again into a living hope!

Note to Self

Dear Self,

The truth you find in the Bible is so much more than good advice; it is good news! The good news of the Kingdom of God is that dead things can be made alive again. Broken relationships can be mended. Sick bodies can be restored. Shattered hearts can be filled with happiness and joy again. When you are facing a dead situation, you can experience incredible growth by accessing resurrection power.

You are capable of more than you realize because Jesus strengthens you. The same Spirit that raised Christ from the dead lives in you, and you can press on in your walk with

Him — not trying to work for more but resting in who Jesus is and what He has done for you!

So, starting today, exercise your faith and see the good things God has in store for your future. Praise Him and thank Him for what He is doing and what He is about to do. Thank Him for divine connections because He is ready and willing to fulfill every desire He has placed within your heart according to His promises. In Christ, you are loved, blessed, made righteous, and poised for a resurrection! Don't work for the victory, but work from victory.

With Love,

Self

61 | The Same Holy Spirit

But if Christ is in you, although the body is dead because of sin, the Spirit is life because of righteousness. If the Spirit of him who raised Jesus from the dead dwells in you, he who raised Christ Jesus from the dead will also give life to your mortal bodies through his Spirit who dwells in you. **Romans 8:10-11**

Do we need help? Absolutely! Our help comes from the Helper, the Holy Spirit.

The same Holy Spirit who helped Jesus carry our shame, who helped Him arise from the grave, and who is alive today, is the same Holy Spirit who is sent to us by Jesus so that we can have the power and authority to overcome our temptations, trials, and tribulations. We can live healed, set free, and empowered to become who God created us to be. But here is the best part: There are only two things we have to do to receive this relationship with the Holy Spirit.

All we have to do is confess with our mouths, by faith, that Jesus is Lord and believe in our hearts that God raised Him from the dead. For it is with our hearts that we believe and are justified, and with our mouths, we are saved and receive the incredible gift of God's Holy Spirit!

Note to Self

Dear Self,

The great foundation of your faith is that Jesus Christ resurrected and reigns as king over the earth and Heaven, death and hell. This resurrection power is the power to cancel your past failures, mistakes, sins, and regrets.

The enemy would love to mess with your faith to the point where you pull back. But, though you live in a fallen world, the Spirit of the Lord is inside of you — the same Spirit that raised Christ from the dead! Therefore, invite the Holy Spirit into the wounded places in your soul. Invite the Holy Spirit through the cracks of your broken heart.

Always remember, the Holy Spirit was left here on earth to lead you into all truth. When you listen and follow the prompting of the Holy Spirit, you won't miss out on opportunities or open doors God sets before you.

With Love,

Self

62 | The Golden Rule

So whatever you wish that others would do to you, do also to them, for this is the Law and the Prophets. **Matthew 7:12**

We want people to treat us the way we want to be treated, rather than how they think we should be treated. The converse is true also. We should treat people how they want to be treated, rather than how we think they should be treated. We live out the Kingdom's principles when we help people by understanding their specific needs rather than giving them what we think they need.

Note to Self

Dear Self,

Let me ask you a few important questions:

- Do you want to be shown honor? Then honor others.
- Do you want grace? Then show grace to others?
- Do you want forgiveness? Then forgive others.

- Do you want to be loved? Then love others the way you want to be loved. Make people feel the way you want to feel.

Therefore, instead of becoming bitter and resentful about how you have been mistreated, choose to do for another what you wished someone had done for you. Use your strength, hope, joy, and love to help them! Make sure the way you treat someone is more of a help than a hindrance, a blessing more than a burden. Every act of kindness to others is an act of kindness to Christ.

Always remember, it is more blessed to give than to receive (Acts 20:35). God did not bless you so that you can sit on what you have. He showed you favor so you can bless others. You will hold back your blessings and the desires of your heart when you become a reservoir instead of a river. Someone needs to be inspired and encouraged by you.

With Love,

Self

63 | Keep Taking Steps

The steps of a man are established by the LORD, when he delights in his way; though he fall, he shall not be cast headlong, for the LORD upholds his hand. **Psalm 37:23–24**

There is no elevator to the top. It's a process, and one step at a time, we will get there. Therefore, we must not quit. We don't need to see the whole staircase to take the next step. We only need to trust the One who sees and knows.

Many of us do not know what God has placed in our hearts to do. But if we believe the scriptures and passages from the Bible, we know He has a journey planned out for us. The key to enduring the journey and reaching our destination is never giving up! It does not matter if we are moving inch by inch or foot by foot. Incremental small steps forward are better than not stepping at all.

Note to Self

Dear Self,

You may have heard others say, "Walk by faith, not by sight" (2 Corinthians 5:7). It's a common phrase and Bible verse used among Christians. But what does it really mean?

To walk by faith is to continue moving forward in the things God has called you to, even when you cannot see a happy ending. It is believing God for good, even when everything around you seems to be evil. Walking by faith means that you trust the Lord so much, you obey, and you step out of your comfort zone to do what He asks, even when you aren't sure what the outcome will be, knowing God will protect you and provide for you. In other words, be determined to keep taking steps forward as God faithfully orders your steps and leads you through the expected and the unexpected.

Have faith the Lord has you on the right path and that He will use every one of your steps for your good, for His Church, and His glory. Each step forward will make you stronger, wiser, more compassionate, and more loving. Keep embracing the adventure of faith because your season of breakthrough and increase is coming as long as you don't give up. You serve a sovereign God who will guide your steps, so put your faith in only Him and live the life He has called you to live!

With Love,

Self

64 | Do Not Hold Back

Be strong and courageous. Do not fear or be in dread of them, for it is the Lord your God who goes with you. He will not leave you or forsake you. **Deuteronomy 31:6**

We can allow the labels that others place on us to define us. We can allow those words and labels to limit us. After all, people constantly put labels on us, telling us what we can and cannot become, what we can or cannot do. People will label us too young, too old, not good enough, too slow, too many mistakes. However, these labels are often not in agreement with what God says about us and our future. God labels us strong, gifted, treasured, more than a conqueror.

Nonetheless, if we don't know any better, we will wear those false labels like they are the truth. The sad thing is that incorrect labels can keep us from our destiny and hold us back. We need to return to the truth of God's Word that will last forever and not meditate on circumstances that will change and fade. It is this truth that enables us to move forward into the future unfazed.

Note to Self

Dear Self,

Let me ask you a few questions:

- Are there labels that are holding you back today?
- Have you ever done something but did not try your best?
- Are you allowing a past failure to hold you back from your purpose?

I'm sorry for all the pain you may have experienced, but you cannot let fear and the labels of others hold you back anymore. It doesn't matter what you've been through; you must push yourself to trust God in everything you do.

When it comes to the promises and the calling God has spoken over your life, don't worry or be dismayed. Let those who doubt you fuel you! Be relentless in achieving your goals, and serve as many people as possible. Be strong and courageous, for the Lord is on your side. Trust God's timing and then live in faith and love.

With Love,

Self

65 | Receiving Your Blessing

Well done, good and faithful servant. You have been faithful over a little; I will set you over much. Enter into the joy of your master. **Matthew 25:23**

There are so many days that come and go when we feel like we cannot catch a break. It seems like everyone around us is being blessed, and we are in the back, trying to find some reason to rejoice. Nevertheless, God is not finished with us yet. His path will lead us to pleasant places. We will be overwhelmed by the privileges that come with following Him, for He has given us a beautiful inheritance.

Note to Self

Dear Self,

When you don't see anything happening, it's easy to assume that what you are waiting for is never coming. But no matter how it looks, God is always behind the scenes working on your behalf. Therefore, please do not give up because you are tired of waiting. God is not finished! The Lord hears your cries, and your blessings are on their way. But while you wait, you have a pivotal part to play in the Kingdom of God, so stay faithful to the process and remain in faith.

How can the Lord forget the beautiful work you have done for Him? He remembers the love you demonstrate as you repeatedly serve His beloved children for the glory of His name. So, don't lose your enthusiasm or allow your heart to grow dull. Follow the example of those who fully received what God has promised because scripture says that you will inherit the blessings of God by faith and patience!

Believe that the Lord is who He says He is and that He will do what He says He will do. Believe in your heart that nothing is too hard for Him! And always remember, Jesus is preparing something extraordinary for everything you have been through.

Lastly, the Lord gracefully gave you gifts and talents as a birthright for you to advance the Kingdom of God, create multiple streams of income, build generational wealth, and empower others to do the same. If you are faithful with the talents and gifts entrusted to you and stay obedient to His Word, I believe the Lord will say, ***"Well done, good and faithful servant. You have been faithful over a little; I will set you over much. Enter into the joy of your master."***

With Love,

Self

66 | Faith and Patience

We do not want you to become lazy, but to imitate those who through faith and patience inherit what has been promised. **Hebrews 6:12**

It's truly unbelievable how impatient our society has become. Financial markets are focused on the next quarter. Fashion markets are focused on the next season. The stock market is focused on the next dollar. Social media influencers are focused on the next post. But in our continual yearning for what's next, we can miss the beauty and gift of the process.

The ideas, dreams, and plans God places in our hearts take time. Sometimes a lot of time. And during all that time, God is working in us so that He can work through us. Our part is to exercise faith and patience in the process.

Faith is believing God, believing He is who He says He is, and He will do what He said He would do. Patience is our capacity to endure the delay, to wait. Also, patience is the ability to see what God is doing in the here and now, to see Him working, moving, and fulfilling His promises in our lives. Therefore, faith and patience is trusting God is good,

God does good, and God knows what He is doing, no matter how long it takes, and no matter what our calling may be.

Note to Self

Dear Self,

When you take your worries to God, you may ask Him to swiftly and painlessly take away your troubles. And, well, sometimes He may do just that. But every so often, God will take you through trials and not around them, and He does so for a reason. Think about it. Who grows stronger? The individual who escapes trouble or the one who gets through it?

Having a challenge doesn't mean God is punishing you. He is growing your faith, which produces patience and develops the strength you need for the fantastic future He has in store for you. God will not let your patience and faithfulness be wasted!

Because of this, you really can have joy in the midst of the trials! You can have peace while you wait! Yes, there will be difficult days. But no matter what you're going through, you can take heart in the promise that Christ is with you, and with faith and patience, you can lack nothing.

With Love,

Self

67 | Prayer: Patience

Heavenly Father,

I praise You for the gift of the Holy Spirit and Your dynamic living Word, which continually molds my soul to mirror Your Son, my King, Jesus Christ. Patience isn't easy, but I thank You for working with me. When life gets complicated, it's hard to submit to the Holy Spirit's power because I want to take control and strive for solutions. Forgive me, Father, for allowing my temperaments to speak first. You love me perfectly and promise to defend me. You hear me and are concerned about me. Help me to trust You completely with my daily battles. From day-to-day, remind me to sit with You and soak in the powerful wisdom available to me.

Please help me to remember Psalm 56 when I am afraid. Periods of waiting often lead me to fear, and fear can chip away at my trust and faith. When days and nights are filled with delay, let Your light of courage find its place within me. Renew within me the calm spirit of hope, joy, and peace. Bless my heart and soul to be established in Christ because through Him, the Kingdom of God is at hand. May I forever be reminded of the sacrifice Jesus made for me and the love

He has for me. The same love that promises never to leave me or forsake me. Please provide the patience I need to pursue the dreams, visions, and plans You placed in my heart.

In Jesus' Name, I pray, Amen.

SELF-REFLECTIONS

Think about the last time you made a decision too quickly—what were the consequences?

_____
_____
_____
_____
_____
_____
_____
_____
_____
_____
_____
_____
_____

68 | Be A History Maker

And I heard the voice of the Lord saying, "Whom shall I send, and who will go for us?" Then I said, "Here I am! Send me. **Isaiah 6:8**

Most people get to watch history; very few get to make it. But we can be among those few history-makers. There is nothing special we have to do for us to be history-makers. We just have to be available and willing to be used by God!

- Moses did not think he was eloquent enough, but he was available and willing.
- Jeremiah thought he was too young, but he was available and willing.
- Gideon thought he was the least, but he was available and willing.
- Esther did not think she could save her people, but she was available and willing.

God is not looking for the strongest, most intelligent, and talented individuals. No, He is looking for people who have a willing heart. He's looking for availability. He is looking for someone who is ready to say, "Here I am, Lord, send me!"

Note to Self

Dear Self,

Will you make yourself available to God today?

The degree to which you are willing to accept your divine assignment is the degree to which God will use you. The Lord is not looking for extraordinary people. He's not looking for the wealthiest, most skilled, gifted, articulate, or educated person in the world. He is looking for an available and willing person.

Therefore, no matter where you've been, what you're afraid of, or what mistakes are in your past, God can still use you to make a difference in this world. What He needs from you is a total commitment to Him. God wants you to be all in on His plans for you. Your relationship with the Lord isn't about your ability; it's about your availability.

If you have a heartfelt readiness to do all you can for the Lord, He will indeed accept your service, and you will be amazed at what He will do in and through you. All you have to do is be willing and committed to doing whatever He wants with your life. Be a history-maker!

With Love,

Self

69 | You Can Do It

Forgetting what is behind and straining toward what is ahead, I press on toward the goal to win the prize for which God has called me heavenward in Christ Jesus. **Philippians 3:13-14**

Let's take a look at a very familiar verse from the book of Philippians: **"I can do all things through Christ who strengthens me." Philippians 4:13**

The Apostle Paul wrote these words while facing some of the worst persecutions of his life. Despite the threat of suffering and death, he understood that the Lord gives us strength in ways that extend beyond the good times and the everything-is-okay moments. Paul understood the authority and peace of Christ could reach right down into his turmoil and discomfort. He learned that Christ would strengthen us through trials and suffering, and He will give us the victory over sin and death.

The reality is, in our walk with Christ, we will go through hard times, and we will be strained. But even during the strain, we can know without a doubt that the Lord is our strength.

Note to Self

Dear Self,

It's no accident that you are here. The Father has chosen you to live in this moment in history because you are preordained to be a part of this generation and to become a history-maker. He has wonderful things for you to do—and only you can do them—right here and right now!

But you need to know that in your walk with Christ, you will go through hard times, and there will be moments when you will feel stressed. But even during stressful moments, you can know without a doubt that Christ is your strength. You can do what the Father has called you to do because everything is possible for those who believe.

Let these Scriptures encourage you further:

- *For by you I can run against a troop, and by my God I can leap over a wall (Psalm 18:29).*
- *But he said, "What is impossible with men is possible with God" (Luke 18:27).*
- *But thanks be to God, who gives us the victory through our Lord Jesus Christ (1 Corinthians 15:57).*

With Love,
Self

70 | Give Me Strength

Oh, guard my soul, and deliver me! Let me not be put to shame, for I take refuge in you. **Psalm 25:20**

Isn't it interesting that we naturally look down at the ground when we're embarrassed, hurting, or uncomfortable? Why is that? Why do we shrink?

We need to always remember that the Lord wants us to keep our heads up! He wants us to walk boldly in Christ. He wants to give us strength in our weakness and help us experience His rest. There is no reason to live ashamed and guilty, afraid to come into the presence of the Lord. We serve a relational, loving heavenly Father who wants us to know that we don't need to look down or be afraid anymore.

Note to Self

Dear Self,

Look up to the Lord who has open arms for you. He knows every second of your past and your future, and He is so in love with you. You have access to a life full of joy and happiness; all you need to do is look up and be strong!

Let us pray:

Heavenly Father,

You are Holy above all others, and all of the strength that I need is within You. I am not asking that You take my trials away. Instead, I ask that Your will be done in my life.

Sometimes I feel like I cannot go on. The pain and fear are too much for me, and I know I do not have the strength on my own to get through it. I know that I can come to You and that You will hear my prayers. I know that it is not Your intent to bring me to this point to leave me alone.

Lord, give me the strength that I need to face today and keep me from making the wrong decisions during my trials. When my child tests me, please give me the strength to respond with wisdom. When I grow irritable, please give me the strength to have insight. When my fury rages, please give me the strength of restraint.

When I become fixed in my ways, please give me the strength to be flexible. When I lose my way, God, please give me the strength to find joy, love, and peace through You. Please help me keep my eyes on You because You are the Holy One, and all of my hope and strength rests in you. Thank you for hearing my prayer.

In Jesus' name. Amen.

Can You Do Me A Favor?

First, if you enjoyed *Soul Care*, would you take a few moments to write a review? Leaving a short review will help me out massively and would be much appreciated.

Secondly, please send a copy of this book if you know someone who needs to be encouraged, inspired, and motivated.

Thirdly, remember, there are blessings that await you when you choose to take a step of faith and move forward! If you are having trouble taking that step forward, please allow me to pray for you. Send me a prayer request so my team and I can join you in prayer: tonywarrick.com/prayerrequest/

Lastly, don't forget to subscribe to my website and catch all my new releases, daily devotionals, and monthly newsletter. You can sign up here: tonywarrick.com

Thank you so much for reading *Soul Care*!

About the Author

Dr. Tony L. Warrick has always had a passion for transformation. This passion unveiled his purpose to see people be all that God has created them to be by connecting the transforming power of Jesus Christ to everyday living.

Born and raised in Washington, D.C., Dr. Warrick overcame incredible odds from his youth by pulling from the grace he experienced during his darkest lessons to help individuals change their lives through spiritual health, personal growth, and professional development. His writings provide daily action steps for every area of a Christian life. It is his aspiration that people are equipped with practical principles to navigate the complex challenges life can bring while moving forward and making a significant impact in their community.

To learn more about Dr. Warrick, please visit: TonyWarrick.com

> twitter.com/IamTonyWarrick
> facebook.com/IamTonyWarrick
> linkedin.com/in/iamtonywarrick

Made in the USA
Middletown, DE
09 April 2023